Shh...

HOW CHILDHOOD SEXUAL ABUSE ALMOST STOLE MY SANITY AND HOW I OVERCAME THE PAST

A MEMOIR BY ANTHEA MCCARTEN

Cover image: Volkan Olmez/Unsplash
ISBN: 9798419158399
Imprint: Independently published

This book was written with the assistance of Your Memoir.
For more information visit yourmemoir.co.uk.
Contact Marnie Summerfield Smith at
marnie@yourmemoir.co.uk or on 07851 548 522

DEDICATION

I dedicate this book to Paul, my husband and my dear children, Luke and Amelia. Paul for his enduring love, loyalty, support and patience. You have encouraged me to step into freedom, uncomplaining whilst I completed my training and wrote my memoirs. Paul, you have waited so long for the day to come when you would see your wife healed from the traumas of her past. Now is our time, the past behind us, the future before us. You are my best friend; my soul mate and I trust you like no other. You have proved yourself to be the best husband.

Luke and Amelia, you are two beautiful souls who have grown into adults your dad and I can be so proud of. You have been through so much but have continued loving me through even the difficult years. I love you so much and treasure our family unit. You both bring joy and meaning to my life. Aim high; I pray you will believe in yourselves as I believe in you for then anything will be possible!

I want to thank Paul's parents; you looked after Paul and especially the children, for without your love, care and self-sacrifice I would have had more worry on my plate throughout those four turbulent years. You are two special individuals with copious amounts of generous acts towards others. I love you!

My foxy family, so many of you, but you all know how much I love, value and treasure you! Thank you for being crazy and keeping me sane, there have been so many tears and heartaches but with fun, laughter and most of all prayer and love, we remain together. Thank you for always believing in me.

Marnie, thank you so much for your endless patience as we worked together to make sure my written memoirs were accurate accounts of my story. We have spent countless hours together and separately on this project and you have been both empathic and kind. We made it!

CONTENTS

PROLOGUE

Freedom

"I didn't want my life to end. I just wanted the pain to end."

In 2002, aged 30, I sat on the windowsill of the spare bedroom of my parents-in-law's home and prepared to jump. I have no recollection of that moment, of wanting to die. But I know that was what I wanted, what I craved in the brief seconds of falling and whatever came next, would be freedom. Freedom from the darkness, freedom from my thoughts and freedom from the pain of living.

Today I know freedom but getting there was a journey – a long one that was not without setbacks. Coaxed from the windowsill and into bed, where my devoted mother-in-law lay with me until the doctor came, I would then spend four years in and out of hospital where I was treated with medication, electroconvulsive therapy (ECT), one-to-one therapeutic counselling, cognitive behavioural therapy (CBT), occupational therapy and psychotherapy. In 2006, I left hospital for the last time, embarked on a further four years of therapy and then undertook four years of training to become a counsellor myself.

In counselling training the significance of needing a good level of emotional intelligence cannot be underestimated. Self-awareness work is a requirement if we are to acknowledge feelings, desires, thoughts and what motivates us to make the choices we do.

I desired freedom! How was I to find freedom? The following questions reveal what my inner dialogue was at the time.

What are my spiritual beliefs other than that of my parents? What motivates me? What are my weaknesses and strengths? How and why do I responded to others the way I do?

Once I connected the dots with the empathic support of my tutors, I was able to change the direction of my life from living in captivity to finding the power to walk, act, speak and live in freedom.

I had been disintegrating, slowly, for 22 years, and it took me eight years of intermittent therapy plus a further four years of counselling training to get well and to become whole again.

Now, in the year 2016, aged 44, as I complete the writing of my story and work as a qualified counsellor, I know that I have found the freedom I craved, although not in the way I thought I would find it when I sat on the window ledge. With therapy supported by prayer, and the support of family and friends, I have found self-acceptance, freedom and am full of hope for the future.

From the age of seven for approximately five years, I was periodically sexually abused by my mother's father. This sustained assault traumatised me and for a long time, defined me. It shaped me into a weak, despairing and introverted girl with no confidence or sense of identity. The actions of the man I refer to only by his initials, DC, were so pervasive that even when by the time I was – to the outside world – a 30-year-old married woman and mother of two, inside I was still a vulnerable, helpless seven-year-old. Not that I knew any of this until I was admitted into hospital. I had no idea of the effect the abuse had had on me.

The suicide attempt was part of me wanting to escape Obsessive Compulsive Thoughts (OCT), which had taken over my life and from which there seemed to be no escape. My OCT, depression, anxiety, lack of confidence were all symptoms of the trauma, but I had pushed through them. For 23 years I ignored the pain that would take me a further 12 years to heal.

37 lost years

I kept telling little Anthea: "You are pathetic, pull yourself together and get on with it."

I didn't want to be that child. I hated her ugliness inside and out, she irritated me, and I wanted to shut her down. But she was there and my trying to eradicate her led to a complete mental breakdown and the first attempt to end my life. I needed to ask that little girl why she was hurting and finally, in therapy, I got a chance to do that. I explored how the abuse had made me feel, how I felt dirty, useless and powerless and how those feelings of guilt and shame had formed my core beliefs – limited self beliefs – beliefs that told me every day I was worthless.

I wanted to be confident and accepted by others as a competent adult, but I was ignoring the part of me that was in a foetal position in the corner of the room – the part of me that felt she had to accept the abuse and couldn't say no. The years of therapy and counselling training enabled me to connect with that inner part of me, I held that little girl and told her, "You're going to be okay. You're safe, you're loved, you're valued, you can do this, and you matter."

I was able to affirm that little girl. I was able to be empathic and kind to her, acknowledging all her pain and insecurities instead of ignoring her. When I began to do that, I began to heal, and I began to feel free. Little Anthea began to uncurl herself from the foetal, mechanism position she was in, no longer needing to self sooth or protect herself from the monster (psychological regression) As I acknowledged the abuse and pain, little Anthea and I became one. Together we are empowered, strong, thriving and healed. Together we live in harmony.

This is the crux of my work and why I am telling my story. To share the message that there is always hope, supporting adult abuse victims and survivors to connect with their inner child, find healing so both adult and inner child can live in harmony. I had to go back and allow that child to heal, otherwise there would have been a part of me that was broken forever. Now I want to help others to do the same.

CHAPTER ONE

I believe that I was able to get to the age of 30 before breaking down because before the abuse, and certainly until I was three, my youngest years were especially happy and secure. I lived in an innocent world; safe and secure, wrapped in cotton wool.

The eldest of four, I was born in 1972 in Kent to Jenny and Roger Fox. Mum, a hardworking housewife, Dad a domestic electrical appliance engineer. My earliest memory is Mum walking me to playschool. My sisters, identical twins Sue and Jo, had been born by then so I would walk to school alongside their buggy. I loved playschool and I loved the journey there, feeling the anticipation of a fun day ahead and wondering which toys had been laid out for us to play with.

The walk seemed to take ages, probably because I couldn't wait to get there, and there was a little alley we had to walk down, which added to the sense of entering a new and exciting world. Our neighbourhood was full of alleyways and as we got older, we played in all of them, much of the time on our bikes. My bike was a beloved blue Raleigh, a second-hand one that my dad did up. My parents had taught me to ride it in our street as there were barely any cars back then.

No childhood is perfect of course. When the twins came along, I felt the loss of Mum's undivided attention. We would go into town and people would stop to coo over and admire my sisters' pretty ginger curls as I stood quietly at the side of the pushchair. For a toddler who, like all egocentric toddlers, believed she was the centre of her parents' world, that was a significant loss. If it hadn't been coupled with what was to come, I might have shrugged it off but as it was, I felt forgotten at times.

There were plenty of good times though. When I was almost eight, my brother Sam was born. I was very happy and would excitedly share with the neighbours "he has red hair!" I was overjoyed to be a big sister again. As a family of six, we weren't rich, so outings usually meant picnics rather than going to restaurants. We liked going to Mote Park in Maidstone to play frisbee, leapfrog and rounders. The beach was a favourite place, as were the woods for tree climbing and walks among bluebells. We would go to our friends' houses to play and there was a group of us who would have colouring competitions. Our Christmases were magic. We believed in Father Christmas and Mum worked hard to give us the best with what Dad brought home. We had food in our bellies, even if that meant Mum going without at times

A lovely part of my childhood was the presence of my Dad's mum who we called Nan Fox. Unfortunately we didn't have contact with Granddad Fox until much later as he and my Nan had separated. Nan Fox's house felt normal. We felt safe, happy and relaxed there, we could be ourselves. She would say, "Sit down and let me read you a story," or, "Do you want to play a game?" We made many happy memories there and never left feeling judged or criticised, only loved and believed in. She was a dream grandparent, and we were very close until her death in March 1990.

Mum's childhood was difficult and her adult relationship with her parents reflected that. But she did her best, sharing with us how determined she was to create a family life that was the opposite of what she had known. She wanted stability and she gave us that. She was a stay-at-home mum, always there to make breakfast, ensuring our uniforms looked smart, collecting us from school and attending important events like sports day. She encouraged us with musical instruments and after school clubs. Tuesday was child benefit day, known to us as Sweeties Day, and we would come home from school and find a Twix in the fridge. I wanted to eat the top layer of caramel first, then the biscuit, but we were told to "eat it properly!" To this day I indulge my inner child by eating the toffee first.

On Tuesdays during the school holidays, we'd all go to the market and then to the Baker's Oven for drink and a cake, so Tuesdays were always the best day of the week. It was, in some ways, a perfect childhood, certainly a perfect home life. We had a routine. Family mealtimes were very important to our parents and at 6pm and not a minute after, we would be sat round that table. Dad would get home at 5.30pm. He would have his cup of tea and a read of the paper while we watched Neighbours, then we'd eat and catch each other up with our days' news.

Mum's background was the old Victorian way of children should be seen and not heard. Dad disagreed and encouraged meaningful discussions round the family meal table, there was lots of laughter too.

My parents have a zany sense of humour! After dinner was cleared away, we'd gather round our parents, sitting on their laps, perhaps one of us playing with Mum's hair.

Unfortunately, I didn't feel I had Mum's support where I needed it the most, a strong, emotional attachment and connection. Seemingly unable to fully receive and accept my love, at times would leave me feeling insecure. I remember one occasion when she was speaking with a neighbour, and I snuggled into her side for a cuddle. She shrugged me off saying, "Get off Anthea, you're always clinging." Mum's acts of rejection were not intentional but more a reflection of her own childhood experiences. In addition, after 5 challenging months of breastfeeding my younger twin sisters she developed postnatal depression.

For many years I felt that I wasn't entitled to ask for a better emotional attachment with Mum because she had been brilliant in so many ways. I didn't want to be ungrateful. However, having had therapy I can now see what my needs were and that they mattered. Also as a result of therapy, I have been able to have meaningful, honest conversations with both my parents about the abuse and my childhood more generally. I have asked my Dad where he felt he made mistakes as a parent. He says that he felt he and Mum were too strict at times.

A few years ago my parents invited us all round for dinner, here they apologised for being overly strict. They also apologised for making us go to church too much. Dad was a deacon at Sittingbourne Pentecostal Church. We would attend two services on a Sunday – morning communion and evening gospel service. Dad attended the monthly church oversight meeting on a Monday. On Tuesdays he and Mum took it in turns to go to a prayer meeting then as I got older, I would babysit, and they would both go. On Wednesday evenings Mum attended a music group and on Thursdays they went to bible study. On Friday evenings we would go to Campaigners Youth Christian Club.

I didn't really need that apology from my parents as I was always happy to go to church. My sisters and younger brother not so much! Saturday was a day off and we generally went to see Nan Fox and/or my mother's parents.

My dad was very much a father of his time. He saw his role as provider and guider and in the beginning wasn't a hands-on dad. He explained that during my early years he wasn't interested in babies and children. He saw my sisters and me as babies who needed feeding one end and cleaning up the other. I know he feels guilty about this, even though he needn't. By the time my brother was born Dad changed and helped Mum far more. Happily, Dad recalls a time when he took me to see his mum and says that's when he fell in love with me. He really enjoyed that one-to-one time. He became a devoted father in later years, but at first, we didn't have a strong bond.

If there hadn't been a sex offender in the family, I would have probably rolled with the punches of my perfectly normal, imperfect childhood as the eldest of four. But DC was watching, and I believe he noticed vulnerability in me, a craving for attention.

When we used to go over to Mum's parents, my sisters and I were very keen to go and play at the park up the road. It was a lovely place, full of trees, flowers and banks where you could hide. At the play park there was a roundabout, swings and a slide, which of course we walked up instead of sliding down. When I was 10, I fell off and landed on my back. Completely winded and unable to move, one of the twins ran back to my grandparents' house and when they returned, my heart sank. I wanted my dad to come and rescue me, be my hero, but instead DC carried me back to his house.

> If someone is giving things to your child or treating them differently to other children in the family, it doesn't mean that they're abusing them but do pay attention. If you notice a change in your child's behaviour, pay attention, especially if that child was bubbly and confident and becomes introverted and shy. We often think there's a problem at school, but it might be closer to home. Statistics from the NSPCC show that in 2019/2020 there were 12,374 sex crimes recorded against children under the age of 10. Reports suggest that 1 in 20 children in the UK have been sexually abused. It is estimated that over 90% of children are abused by someone they know. The problem is much bigger than shown in official statistics, most children don't tell anyone that they're being sexually abused. It's a crime that is usually only witnessed by the abuser and victim.

I was gutted. By this time, DC was already abusing me, I was disempowered, used to hiding my feelings and unable to voice that I wanted my dad. Maybe he'd offered but been shouted down by DC wanting to ingratiate himself with me or suppress my father. Either way it was another hurt that I repressed.

DC groomed me from an early age. A pound note would be taped inside my birthday cards when the twins only got 50p. Later they would get a pound note and I would receive a fiver. One Christmas I received a record player, which was much more generous than the twins' gifts. They noticed this, of course and would comment. There were other occasions when DC would slip me a 50p and say, "Don't tell your sisters."

CHAPTER TWO

I lay in the dark listening to the twins' breathing. They had gone out like lights, tired from the later than usual bedtime. My parents were out, and my grandparents were babysitting. I hugged my legs to my chest and felt drowsiness begin to take me. Then, a noise. Adrenaline flooded me. Was it? No. It couldn't be. Yes, it was. A footstep. Someone was coming upstairs. There was no reason for anyone to do so. The toilet was downstairs, and we children were as quiet as mice. Was it DC? I hoped against hope that it was Nan. I heard another step, then another. Heavy feet. I knew then. I was alone and he was coming for me.

My heart began to race. Please God, no.

I squeezed my eyes shut, then opened them again, desperately hoping I had imagined the sound. Another step. I pulled the covers over my head. I held my breath. I could hear my heart. Was he coming into the bedroom? Was he going to do it again? Please God, don't let him touch me. Please, please, please. Thump went the stairs. Thump went my heart. Fear engulfed me and I thought my heart was going to burst out of my tiny chest. I peeked out from under my duvet. The door opened and I saw the light from the landing seep into the room. Then to my horror, DC's familiar shape followed it. Terror gripped me. I was still not breathing and now I was sweating. No one could protect me now. Please God! I could hear him getting nearer. He was next to me. I could smell him. I didn't move a muscle. He crouched down. His face was next to mine. I stared at him. Something glinted.

"Fifty pence," he said, holding up a coin. "Don't tell your sisters." There was a pause. He smiled at me. I took the coin. Then he stood up and left. I watched the door close and breathed a sigh of relief. I had escaped, for tonight at least. I tucked the money under my pillow and lay still. My heart slowed. Thank you, God. I had escaped. For now. A single, hot tear escaped my eye and ran onto the pillow.

The panic a child experiences, living in dread, not knowing when, and if, they're going to be abused every time they are with the abuser is an indescribable fear. It wasn't until I came across complex trauma in my counselling studies that I realised the destructive impact it had had in all aspects of my development growing up. As victims/survivors, for various reasons, can underestimate the effects of abuse but in my case complex trauma came within a hair's breadth of killing me.

Of course to DC, this was an opportunity for him to groom me. Not that this was a well-known phrase in those days. That 50p was silence money. He knew absolutely that what he was doing was wrong. And it was so confusing. We didn't have much materially, which he knew, and gifts were gratefully received.

I wasn't receptive to the abuse, but I was receptive to the time he gave me. Young children can be totally egocentric. Everything is about them and on an innate level they understand that they need adult contact for their physical and emotional development. Of course what DC did affected my emotional development in the most negative way possible, but as a child, I didn't understand this, believing I was to blame and powerless to stop it.

Fortunately my grandparents were rarely asked to babysit as my parents didn't go out much. But DC and Nan would take us three girls, before Sam was old enough, on camping trips. What could have been more normal and seemingly generous? I'm sure my parents appreciated the break like any normal people would. But the trip was far from normal. DC dictated the sleeping positions, ensuring that I was next to him. Although I don't have clear memories of many of the occasions of abuse, I do remember a camping trip. When everyone was asleep, he began touching me. It felt like it went on forever, but it was probably only a few minutes before thankfully, one of the twins woke up and wanted the toilet.

"We'll all go, we'll all go," DC said, and he took me by the hand as the five of us walked to the toilet block. I remember his grip. It was very tight on my small hand. Was he frightened? Was he keeping me with him for fear that I might say something? To the best of my recollection, the abuse started when I was seven, and stopped when I was about 12. The majority of it happened on camping trips and fishing trips but also in the front room of Nan and DC's house.

I believe I was seven when the abuse started because that's when I started to feel different. It is also when my parents noticed a difference in me too. I had always gone off to school feeling happy. Mum recalls how, the day I started school, I skipped away from her without even looking back. Then, when the abuse began, my school reports began to say, "Anthea is shy, Anthea should take part more and raise her hand and answer questions, Anthea is in a daydream world most of the time." One comment was, "If she spent as much time concentrating on her work as she does gazing out the window, she would do better."

Seeing on my school reports that from the age of seven the once bubbly girl became shy, spending more time gazing out the window, was confirmation to me that the abuse had begun. I couldn't focus on the here and now because it was too painful, and I was trying to escape from reality. I would take myself somewhere, an imaginary place, so I could feel safe. I got the nickname "square eyes" because I loved the television so much. It's quite common in abuse victims to find watching television a form of escapism. Black and white movies were my favourites.

Believing I was the only one being abused, made me feel isolated, lonely and abandoned. It was a pain that I had to face alone. Some of my early years needs of complete safety and security were no longer being met and my still-forming boundaries were shattered leaving me feeling unsafe in the world. The abuse and the keeping quiet about it damaged me in equal measure. I was completely robbed of innocence and was no longer carefree.

My confidence began to suffer. In our classroom we had individual trays into which the teacher would put the book she had selected for us. I loved reading and was always excited to see which book I was going to read next. Then all of a sudden, I was petrified of walking up to my tray. I feared what was inside. I feared being asked to answer a times table question. I was anxious and nervous; I knew I would not be able to achieve.

I had been happy and confidently able to speak to a grown up, asking for my basic needs to be met: a cuddle, a drink or something to eat. "Teacher, can I go to the toilet please?" and "Can you help me with this piece of work?" These were easy questions for me then – boom! All the above seemed difficult. I wondered if caregivers would be displeased with me. Would they reject my requests or just find me plain annoying?

I wanted to disappear. I wanted to be invisible. I felt I couldn't do things anymore, that I would sound stupid. Nothing in my world was sure anymore. I felt bad, dirty and guilty and it became my core belief system that I was in fact bad, dirty and guilty. I had always been told that I was a good girl, and my parents were often complimented on how well I behaved. Suddenly I felt this was no longer true. I felt that I had done something terrible, but I didn't know what it was. The fear of being found out was all-consuming. There was so much shame.

I wasn't that interested in fishing, but I went because DC asked me. This was someone I loved and even though I feared the worst, I wanted to believe the best of him. This is the confusion for victims, especially since most children know their abusers. Children want, and actually on a basic level need, to believe that adults will change; that the adults who hurt them actually love them. This is why in the most horrific child-abuse cases, children often still say that they want to stay with their abuser. Children need to believe and trust adults because they are meant to provide our safety, ensure our survival and provide our learning in the world.

I was in a world of confusion and a great deal of my time was absorbed by that. That's why I started to fail at school. DC introduced me to a confusing adult world that a child should not be introduced to. I was aware of things that I shouldn't have been made aware of – secrets of adult sexuality. A child can't deal with that. I was powerless. Children need positive touch from their caregivers to encourage the physical and psychological development of the brain but what I experienced was not positive touch.

I watched a documentary about a woman who had suffered abused as a child and she explained, "Our bodies are designed to respond to touch. This is not your guilt. This is not your shame to own. Your body did what your body is supposed to do: respond to touch, even if it is a negative one."

This wasn't my experience but for those who experience this, the shame is immense. I had my own sense of shame, and it was growing.

But despite this, I wanted to believe that DC really loved me and was choosing to spend time with me. I wanted to think he singled me out because I was his favourite not because he wanted to use me. Knowing I was his favourite made me feel that I mattered. I felt special. And I can recall happy times on the fishing trips as well as traumatic times. In the 24 hours that we might be away together, the abuse – in terms of the time it took – was a small part, and I enjoyed much of the rest of it.

That said, when the abuse happened, it seemed to take forever. I felt as if time had stood still. Most times it was dark, and my only feeling was that I was desperate for it to be over. I would be frozen, desperate for it to stop. How many minutes? I have no idea. Time is distorted during trauma and your body's survival instincts take over. I liken this to being on a ride somewhere like Alton Towers. It's over in a flash, isn't it? Fun seems to be over in a flash, pain lasts an eternity.

My response was to freeze, research has shown this is common, I was a small child, he was a grown man, I was helpless, no strength to fight or flight and anyway, escape was impossible. When we are under attack our automatic survival instincts kick in – fight, flight or freeze;

> My parents never sat us down and told us about the birds and the bees. Mum was quite a prude back then. I never saw my parents naked in the bath. When we went swimming Dad would take Sam into the men's changing room and we'd go off with Mum; we were all quite shy about seeing each other in the buff. We knocked on doors and respected each other's privacy. As a young parent living with shame and raising small children, I struggled to be relaxed around the kids seeing me naked, but my goal was to protect them, so I spoke with Luke and Amelia about safe boundaries and how they can be the boss of their own bodies.
>
> It was summer, the paddling pool was out. I was sunbathing and they were playing. They came and laid on the towel next to me and I spoke with them. I explained that they are in control of all parts of their bodies being touched and that "no means no". I went on to say that if anyone did try to touch their penis or vagina or anywhere where they did not want to be touched to either tell us or a trusted adult. We need to give our children the vocabulary to understand and maintain safe boundaries. Establishing trust with a child empowers them and they will feel more able to tell you if someone breaks their boundaries. In my early life, I had no idea what was happening or how to articulate it. Children should also be taught the real names for their private parts. This teaches them there is no shame in connection with their sexuality. Nicknames are fine as long as children know there is no shame when we use the correct terms too.

and until we're in that situation we don't know which of those three things we will do. My survival instinct was to freeze, not a chosen response, this is important to remember. My instincts were telling me what was happening was wrong, but I was trapped, like a rabbit in headlights. Freezing was the best way my small body knew how to protect me from the trauma. I tried pretending to be asleep and I remember thinking, I don't want him to know that I'm awake. I don't want him to think that I'm agreeing to this. I thought that if he knew

I was awake and not stopping him, that it might give him the okay to continue. However, he sometimes abused me when I was awake. He would put his hand down my top when we were in the fishing tent. But I just coped as best I could each time it happened. What else could I do?

CHAPTER THREE

"Granddad!"

The hiss of his name escaped my lips before I knew it. I was 12 and we were in DC's lounge on one of our regular Saturday visits. The room was full of people, the TV was on with the football scores being announced, and the air was thick with cigarette smoke. I was sitting on DC's lap and as he reached for me, inside I screamed: No! No! Please God. No! What if someone notices? I couldn't believe that I was no longer safe even with all my family in the room. The horror that what he was doing would be discovered was overwhelming. I was the one who was scared about other adults noticing, not him, and in that moment, the fear someone would see what he was doing was stronger than my fear of telling him no. It was the first time I'd ever spoken out.

"Shh," he said. And that was that. He never tried again. It's as if he thought I was finding my voice, and for once he was scared. Why did I, and why do other victims stay silent for so many years? In my case the abuse was quite sporadic, so there would be moments when I thought it was over. And there were happy times. Nan would occasionally take us to the sweet shop, or we'd laze in their garden on a sunny day whilst the adults were indoors. These were happy times. And I would sometimes watch DC working in his shed.

I really loved and looked up to him. I wanted to hold onto the happy times more than the sad and confusing times. But there came that tipping point where I couldn't cope anymore; cope with covering for him and trying to hide what he was doing. The fear and shame was too much for me to hold. But in the end, that day in the lounge when I stopped the abuse and where I used to feel shame, I now feel proud that I found the courage to put a stop to an adult sexually assaulting me. My voice was small. It was just a whisper – but it was powerful!

After the abuse was revealed, extended family members would ask why I didn't tell and why I hadn't said no. As far as I knew they never asked DC why he had sexually assaulted me. Our culture is still, maybe more than ever, focused on victim-shaming. Still rape victims are asked why they wore what they wore, drank what they drank, and why they walked alone in the dark. Why didn't you NOT rape that person? That must always be the question.

"If Anthea didn't like it, she could have said no." This was a line that I heard again and again. It's extraordinary that people would go as far as admitting that it might have happened and that this was okay but what was not okay was that I didn't stop it. Victim blaming at its finest and most gruesome.

I think it's really important to explain that abused children feel an overwhelming sense of shame and guilt for what has happened and for not speaking out. I was afraid that if I disclosed what was going on, I would be perceived as the troublemaker and accused of being responsible for a split in the family. I was afraid that DC would no longer love me, that I would no longer be his favourite. I was afraid of rejection. It's vital to remember that we are dealing with children who are still developing, and who do not yet have emotional maturity. For example in my case, the attention outside of the abuse that DC was giving me made me feel special. I was completely naïve and craving attention, probably a result of Dad not being too interested in me in my early years and having adorable baby twin sisters that Mum was understandably busy with.

Every little girl's dream is to be at the centre of their daddy's world. Today, all three of us girls know that we are our daddy's world. He describes us as his flowers and feels angry at those who have wronged us. He feels that these people have tried to crush his flowers. But when I was small, I was seeking that male attention. Sadly, being sexually abused came with the attention I was getting, but I tried to dismiss that part and pretend it wasn't happening.

CHAPTER FOUR

I didn't know that the occasion in the lounge would be the last time that DC would abuse me and that it would take another three years, and for me to reach the age of 15, before I told anyone. The person I told was my sister Jo. I think I was just so frightened that it was going to happen again and the further away it was in time, the more I wanted to believe I had escaped it and the more the fear that I might not have done, increased. Another camping trip was being planned and I was terrified.

It was the school summer holidays of 1987. I can't remember exactly what I said although I wasn't explicit in detail, but we were alone in our bedroom and I said something like, "Granddad touched me." Jo immediately believed me. I've never forgotten this because I was terrified that she wouldn't.

"Mum and Dad should know," she said. That was Jo, trying to do the sensible thing. I must have been drawn to telling her for that reason. It was quite a short conversation, but Jo took complete control, even though she was only 13. As I recall those memories, I feel proud. Now I'm okay about what happened but when I think about her belief, love, and maturity at a time when I was lost and hurting so badly, I feel overwhelmed and full of love for her. Jo was friends with the daughter of our church pastor, and she suggested we tell her so that she could tell her father. I was comfortable with that. It wasn't as scary as us going straight to an adult and within a few days of my telling Jo, the pastor's daughter knew. The next thing I remember is being at his house after a Sunday evening church service.

"I think your parents should know about this," he said. "Do you agree?" I did agree. I needed them to know because the burden of keeping DC's secret was too much. Pastor suggested three options: that I could tell my parents myself, that he could tell them for me, or that we could tell them together. I opted for us to tell them together and Pastor took me home, then we sat with Mum and Dad.

They listened, then they looked at me and asked me just the once if it was true. "Yes, "I said. "It's true." The four of us sat together in shock. Dad says he felt shocked to the core, could hardly take it in and had no idea how to deal with such devastating news. He made it his mission to ensure the planned holiday was cancelled. My parents told me I would not have to deal with the situation anymore. Dad told me that he did not want me to fear DC or to fear that the abuse would ever happen again.

The pastor recently reminded me that he had informed us of our options, that we could go to the police, and what it would potentially mean for me if the case went to court. I didn't want to take that route.

I was frightened when Pastor left. He had been a support to me and although Mum and Dad believed me, I didn't know how they were going to react. But nothing happened and I went to bed. It was a devastating, sad time for all of us. I didn't cry that night. I felt numb and exhausted. I had cried many other nights and I cried with Jo, and the pastor, but not with Mum and Dad. I think I wanted to protect them from seeing me broken. They sent me to stay with Grandad Fox for a week.

Dad recorded the events of the next week in his diary. Reading it recently, he told me, "Oh, Amf, as I am typing this I am cringing at the immaturity and religiosity of it. It is painful to copy it out. Oh how I crave for my time over again. How it would be different now."

We can all judge ourselves harshly with the benefit of hindsight, and my dad's outlook has changed on many things, so I really appreciate him allowing me to share his private diaries:

> August 4, 1987: Oh, but I have a problem today, Lord. You know it Father. I don't feel I can even write it down here. You said in your word: Cast all your cares upon Him for He cares for you. Oh Father, please give me strength to deal with it, or take the problem away. Thank you, Lord. Amen.
>
> August 10, 1987: Father, all that word entails. The problem I had on the 4th is still there (like it was going to go away?!) and today is Monday. Father-in-law has been molesting Anthea on outings etc. The result is that now Anthea is very distressed. (It) has affected (Jen) rather badly. Today I have planned to go and see father-in-law at work, so mother-in-law does not find out. What an irksome task I have to perform. I am not looking forward to it at all! I come to pray and seek your face on the matter.
>
> Things to say this afternoon:
>
> - You have been doing things you should not to Anthea
> - Her Christian life is declining (I don't think I said this)

- Please don't ask the girls to stay anymore
- We forgive you
- We love you
- I have decided to see you first to decide on the next course of action

The meeting went without too much trauma, but he denied it all. He said, 'Anthea shouldn't be so silly,' etc. However (apart from that we forgive him) I did say most of all I had planned to say, and yes, I did feel the Lord was with me and in that I did not come away scarred and with my tail between my legs as I have at other occasions. Praise the Lord. Whatever the outcome of all this I can respect myself as a parent!

Reading Dad's diaries it was clear that they were putting my grandmother's needs first to avoid her being hurt. That's why the decision was made for my dad to see DC at the school where he would be on his own in his caretaker's office. Mum's diaries back this up:

> August 9, 1987: Dear Lord, You know the plight that has come upon our family. I feel torn and numb inside. How often we read of this sort of thing happening in other families, and now it happened in ours. Oh, Lord, these past two or three days have been awful. I just pray that somehow You will work all things together for good (these words taken from a verse in the Bible). Precious, Lord, I do praise You that things didn't go further than they did. (Mum explained recently that what she meant here was that it wasn't sexual intercourse). Thank You that you only allow the hand of Satan to go so far. (I must add here, DC was in complete control, there were no other forces at play, and it was his choice to molest me. Mum added recently: even at this point I was trying to look at the positives of this dreadful act, but in no way was I feeling that what he had done wasn't bad enough).
>
> I pray for Rog as he goes to see Dad on Monday. I'm absolutely dreading it. We don't know how he is going to react. I honestly think this is the worst thing I have ever encountered in my life. I pray that Mum would be protected from ever finding out, it would finish her completely. Dad is all she has. Maybe, at some time, Dad will tell her himself, that's up to him. From my point of view, Lord, I can honestly say I don't feel any anger towards Dad, only love. I feel I really want to help him. I pray that there will be an opportunity to show that love, in spite of what has happened.

As I was writing this book and showing Mum these diary entries I was including, she said, "It makes me feel sick that I wrote these words back then. I feel like an awful person, and I simply cannot understand so many of the decisions that I made. But after having had counselling with Family Matters a few years later, I now understand why I did what I did."

Later Mum told me, "My pastor brought a basket of stones to a service and invited each of us to take a stone. He said it could represent anything we liked. I chose for the stone to represent all the pain that DC has caused our family; from Anthea and her siblings who were affected by this, myself and Roger, Paul and the children; the whole family. I still have that stone and when DC dies, I plan to put it in his hand, and he can take all the pain away with him."

On the day that Dad went to see DC, Mum stayed home with me, and we were all very, very nervous. Nan Fox had come to stay for moral support. Dad told DC that we would not be going on the camping trip with him and that he would never be left alone with us girls again. DC went home and told my grandmother that he'd been "falsely accused" of molesting me.

On August 12, Mum wrote in her diary:

> Dear Lord, I just want to thank You. Mum rang me last night; Dad has told her about the incident. She feels like we did, numbed. I thank You that I was able to talk to her and tell her that we love them both. It's hard, Lord, because I don't want to hurt either of them, and yet I know that this must be hurting terribly. I pray that You will sustain Mum through this, and I pray most of all (if he hasn't yet) that Dad will own up and confess. Oh, Lord, I do pray in Jesus's name, turn this evil thing to work for good, as according to Your Word.

You can see my mum struggling here, conflicted. Her mum struggled to believe her, as did other members of the family. Mum simply repeated, "We believe her. We believe her. She's our daughter, we believe her."

Finally, my parents went to see Nan and DC together and DC said several things: that I was silly, but also that it was innocent and unintentional. He then went on to explain that he had only been playing smacking and tickling games with me.

I remember my parents coming home and breaking the news. "He has admitted it!" Dad said. I was shocked. Then I was elated. But my relief was only to last a couple of seconds before they went on to explain that DC told them, "I didn't know it was making her feel uncomfortable. I was only playing and if I touched her anywhere, I shouldn't have then it wasn't on purpose. Thank you for bringing it to my awareness because it means that I can be more aware with other children, so it won't happen again."

I couldn't see it at the time, but this man had not only manipulated, conditioned and controlled me, now he was exerting his power again by manipulating and controlling my parents. Inside I was screaming. But that wasn't it. That wasn't it! I knew that what he had done was not an accident or an innocent, unintentional touch. I knew that much, especially aged 15. DC knew I was unable to articulate the specifics of the molestation, and that I would be too embarrassed to explain exactly what he'd done and where. That day he made it our dirty secret. Everyone else would wonder, doubt even about what really happened but only he and I would know the truth. His hand over my mouth felt ever tighter. It was clever how he got himself off the hook that day. In my mind I remember going over and over what he had done to try and validate to myself: "No, this happened to me, this hurts, that was wrong." I

> Research shows it is common for perpetrators to undertake smacking and tickling games. This doesn't mean that all adults who smack and tickle are abusers. But perpetrators can use this as a means to touch inappropriately under an apparently innocent guise. There is a video of DC giving me a much-wanted body warmer for my birthday. I go to hug him to say thank you and he slaps me on the bottom.
>
> It may seem strange to hear it now but in the culture of the 1980s no one thought much about it. Seemingly, there wasn't the awareness of appropriate and inappropriate behaviour and compared to today, society still felt overwhelmingly sexist. The media's response to feminism was not a positive one; all this talk of freedom is making you unstable, no one will want to marry you, go home, put up, shut up and cook our dinner and all will be well.
>
> We need to teach our children that it's okay to tell an adult if they don't like something, if they don't want to hug, kiss or sit on someone's knee. I have heard parents say, "Give such-and-such a kiss goodbye," when a child is clearly reluctant. It's not that the person they're not wanting to kiss is an abuser, but we need to let our children develop boundaries, feel empowered to be able to say no and know that they can refuse physical contact. They shouldn't be told to do something just because it's polite. This gift of empowerment builds a bond of trust between you and them and prepares them for the big wide world

recalled the fishing trips, the camping trips, what happened when I sat on his lap.

I had been silenced and disempowered. I felt numb, then devastated that his lies were being believed. I felt powerless, not least because I could see that Mum was relieved that maybe it hadn't been intentional abuse and that she'd be able to maintain her relationship with her parents. I had been groomed, abused and silenced and worse was to come.

CHAPTER FIVE

"Sorry if I've ever hurt you."

Acid burned in my throat, and I thought I was going to be sick. It was the first time I had seen DC since I disclosed the abuse and he had managed to trap me in the porch to, "talk to me privately". I stared at the floor. IF? I thought. IF? The seconds ticked by. Did he expect me to speak? Did he want me to tell him it was okay? My heart was racing, and my palms pricked with sweat. "That's okay," I said. He leaned in for a kiss and hug goodbye, opened the door and left. I leaned against the cool glass, gulping the air. How had I ended up in this situation?

After the abuse was revealed, there was a short time when we didn't see DC. This was mainly because of animosity from some members of my mum's family. There was one conversation when one of them said to my dad, "But this is MY dad we're talking about." Dad responded, "Yes, and this is MY daughter."

But before long things slipped back to the way they were – a fake, phoney life of dutiful visits, cups of tea, family functions and smiley photographs. I don't remember being asked or not asked if I wanted to visit DC. The fact is that I should simply have not been put in that situation. But I was and I felt that I had to try and continue as normally as I could even though I was petrified.

There would be vivid flashbacks every time I saw him and when DC embraced me, I'd relive the abuse and freeze. His hands were a trigger and I felt physically sick every time I saw them and remembered what they had done. Another trigger was a battery-operated talking fish on the lounge wall. Everyone was oblivious and would laugh at this fish and I would go along with it while sickening thoughts of him with his hands down my top on Deal pier coursed through my mind. The smell of the house, certain conversations, even songs, they were all painful reminders. I couldn't escape.

No one, including me, knew what a trigger was or what it meant. No one noticed my pain. I should never have been in DC's company again but most Saturdays and on countless other occasions I would face the man who had abused me. I was expected to forget what he had done and just get on with it.

"We are never going to talk about this again. We are going to carry on as normal." No one ever spoke those words but that's what happened. No one said a thing about what had happened to me. My parents are full of regret, full of needless guilt. Dad told me, "If I had my time back, I would make sure you had never clapped eyes on that man again after what he did to you."

But it was DC who caused this and DC who victimised me and everyone around me. Many people have suffered as a result of his actions. He threw the stone into the water and from it ripples of pain spread far and wide. Mum didn't know how to deal with what her father had done. Dad felt very much that this was on his shoulders as the man of the family. He's a quiet man, my father, but he has inner strength. He's strong but not in a bolshie, physical way. He's not one for conflicts and confrontations but he can't stand bullies and DC was a bully. Dad was very much controlled and manipulated by the whole situation.

A grandfather is somebody who is meant to be a role model, someone you put on a pedestal. A grandfather is somebody who is meant to keep you safe and love you unconditionally. For me, this belief was crushed, not overnight – it was a gradual process over some years. It would have started the first time he abused me and that first time, there would have been a part of me that thought that was it, a one off. But then when the abuse did happen again, the fear began. I was filled with panic every time I saw him, how can I protect myself? A sense of dread entered my life.

I started living in a trauma state wondering every time he visited or when we visited them, whether there would be a touch. My innocent child's mind found this impossible to process. It was a corrupt adult world, and I could not navigate my way through it. And even in my adult life, when he was visiting me in hospital during my breakdown, I still didn't want to dismiss the man I called Grandad, even though I slowly realised that I wasn't truly loved by him. It had been a conditional love. DC was only making me feel special so he could get what he wanted. I was of no value to him at all.

That was the most upsetting revelation for me. I really thought DC loved me, but he didn't. He just wanted his own self-gratification, so I grieved for the loss of an important relationship with a man I needed to love and trust.

Our Christian upbringing was largely about forgiveness and our naïve interpretation of that was to continue on as normal. I can see from my parents' diary entries that forgiving DC was high on their list of priorities. I was expected to do the same. We thought it was our responsibility to reassure whoever had wronged us and to tell them we forgave them and loved them. But in doing that, I invalidated my own pain. Other people were invalidating my pain too, but mainly I was – although I wouldn't have known how to articulate that. And how could I forgive someone when they hadn't even admitted that they had wronged me? It was a struggle and all I knew to do was to behave the way others expected me to behave, which was to continue to go to my grandparents' house.

Looking back I now know I was depressed. The police have my diaries from when I was younger, but I have the ones I kept in my teenage years. From the age of 14 to 16, and even up to 18, there are quite a few entries where I wrote, "I feel really sad today, but I don't know why." Our pastor at the time tried to support me as best he could by organising some pastoral care. There were a couple of ladies at the church, and he asked me which one I would like to talk to. I chose a lady with whom I already had a bond and as I got older, I used to go and stay with her. But I never received any counselling or professional support. I don't blame that on the adults around me as awareness and available professional help was relatively unknown in the 1980s. While this lovely lady was excellent at listening and giving me spiritual support, what I needed was professional help. The sessions with her went on for a few months but she had little knowledge of the consequences and impacts of sexual abuse.

The topic of sexual abuse can cause some listeners to feel uncomfortable, they may not know what to say, and as a victim I tried to avoid the topic too. What had happened caused me to feel extremely self-conscious. Reliving it only increased the shame I felt. Talking about the abuse was a trigger for the trauma I was trying to blot out.

The word abuse either wasn't used or I didn't hear it. On the rare occasions the situation was mentioned, people used a lot of euphemistic language and I followed suit saying that DC had "touched me inappropriately", "somewhere he shouldn't." I was 18 when I first heard the word abuse; a dear friend of mine, Maria, used it in connection with what had happened to me, and it hit me really hard and took time for me to digest.

For many years up to when I married and beyond, I felt I had to continue doing what was expected of me. I continuously felt blame, guilt and shame around my mum and her family. The six of us were ostracised from many parts of the family who were told that I was a liar. This compounded my belief that I was a bad child. It was another building block to add to the list of Negative Automatic Thoughts (NATS) that were steadily growing inside me.

I know and understand the vulnerabilities of a child and the importance of love, guidance and nurture. And as a parent I realise how difficult it can be to raise healthy souls and minds of little ones. My personal experience is that there were some testing times as Paul and I tried to raise children who, one day, would be shaped into independent, fully functioning individuals, able to interact with a healthy attitude towards others.

We tried daily to support their process and perceptions of the world and concepts such as fear, pain, consequences, success, failure, joy, love and safety.

Because of the abuse, there were disruptions to my mental and emotional development which defined who I became as a child and as an adult. I was left feeling unsafe, confused, unsure, insignificant, a spectator of the world rather than part of it.

CHAPTER SIX

"I would have reported it to the police."

"I would have beaten him to a pulp."

"I would have stopped you from seeing him."

These are some of the things people have told me they would have done if I was their child. But there is no handbook for the painful situation that we as a family found ourselves living through. Our attempt at coping was influenced hugely by our faith and my mum's pursuit of her then dysfunctional relationship with her parents.

In recent years I have been incredibly fortunate to have had some very honest and soul searching conversations with Mum. We had to do it as after the abuse was revealed our relationship had really disintegrated and I felt an anger and resentment that at times was almost overwhelming. Mum put our disconnect down to a personality clash but there was clearly more to it than that. I feel that I reminded Mum of herself when she was young, that I brought up her own, locked away childhood pain. I felt that I was who she used to be at home, which was insecure, needy, good, sweet, compliant, and adaptive.

Among the four of us children, my nickname was Sunshine Bum! This was because where my siblings rebelled against our strict environment, I feared consequences and craved acceptance. Despite feeling anxious and walking on eggshells at times, it seemed a safer option to conform to not make anyone angry or be the cause of bad feelings. I became an expert at mimicking adult behaviour: trying not to say anything silly, being helpful, listening to adults, and not being angry. Basically, I was a people pleaser.

As the first born, I had Mum all to myself for three wonderful years. According to John Bowlby, the psychologist who did pioneering work in child development and attachment theory, this was extremely valuable to my development. Mum breastfed me and I know we had a close bond. The birth of the twins and her subsequent postnatal depression affected us. I wasn't getting the attention I craved. I became extremely insecure, and this was exacerbated when the abuse began and my world as I knew it, collapsed.

I felt that I was being dismissed, even if it wasn't the case. When I watch old family videos, you can see me act out so as to be noticed. You can hear my parents saying, "Oh, stop it, Anthea!" and "Get out the way, Anthea!" Dad would be filming the twins and Sam doing cartwheels and I would try to get in and copy everyone and shout, "Watch me, Daddy, watch me!" I was seeking attention and reassurance. In the same way that babies cry because they need something, I was trying to get attention because something was wrong. I wanted protection and this behaviour was me crying out: Look at me, notice me, I'm hurting, I need comfort, reassurance that I am not bad but worthy of your time, love and attention.

At the time I wondered why my parents didn't want to film me. This, of course, wasn't the case. There are plenty of old films of me but those were my NATs. I was hitting the self-destruct button, punishing myself because I believed I was a horrible child. I told myself that no one wanted me around, that I was a pest, an irritation. When I watch those videos today, I feel both sad and happy. I feel sad for that little girl, but I don't feel like it's me I'm watching because I no longer seek validation of how others feel about me. It's as if I am watching someone else and I want to reach out to hug her. This wasn't always the case. When I was ignoring my inner child, videos and old family photos made me cringe. Now I metaphorically hold her, nurture her and am filled with love and compassion. She no longer irritates or annoys me. Where I only ever saw a child who was ugly, weak and pathetic, now I see someone beautiful. I admire her courage and strength, her bravery, her survival instincts and her quiet fighting spirit.

There were many times when I was young when I tried to reach out and was told, "Stop clinging, Anthea!" Dad even wrote in his diary:

> Dear Lord, what can I do for Anthea other than pray? There is only prayer. Anthea needs deliverance, where can I go to for help? She clings to me, sometimes embarrassingly so, it's as though she craves love. She says older men frighten her because of what happened, she obviously trusts me and Mum. Why does she always want me and Jen to cuddle her? Is it because she wants to know she can trust? Anthea is emotionally damaged. She wants to feel the assurance everything is okay, to crush the guilt, to gain acceptance that she is forgiven.

I believe I developed a sense of abandonment at two stages in my life – the first when the twins were born and the second when the abuse began, and I was under attack and unprotected. I began to believe that the feelings of my mum and siblings were more important than mine. I am not worthy of all these things, I told myself. The emotional needs of others matter more than yours, Anthea. I didn't know how to validate my own pain and how to self-care or self-sooth when I felt overwhelmed by feelings of rejection.

The only way I could survive was to mask my own inner turmoil and carry on in the ways that I felt others expected. I was aware that the abuse had caused Mum pain and also that she was hurting due to her difficult relationship with her parents. How could I reveal my pain when Mum carried so much pain too? That would make me selfish, wouldn't it? That's what I thought. I felt that my purpose was to be used, not loved, and this greatly contributed to the loss of confidence and self-worth.

As the years went on, I began to resent Mum, believing she had emotionally withdrawn from me. I found myself rejecting Mum's love and thinking that I didn't need or want it. I thought that if she really loved me, she would reject her father and then we would be okay. I convinced myself I didn't need to be emotionally attached to Mum. I was in denial. I did crave a deeper connection with Mum but knew it couldn't happen all the while DC was still in her life. It hurt too much. I felt that although I was believed, what he had done to me still wasn't being completely validated by the one person who mattered most. I didn't like how Mum craved an emotional connection with him. That hurt. I resented it, and I needed her to crave that connection with me. I drip-fed things about the abuse, hoping that the more Mum knew, her decision to continue loving him might be swayed.

The Christmas following the summer I disclosed the abuse, I began writing in my first diary. The police have these as many entries were about the abuse. I also wrote about my relationship with Mum, my parents, friends and later Paul and God. I hid it in my wardrobe. I would sit on my bed and write it in the evenings before going to sleep. There were strict bedtimes, and I would go to my room, read the Bible, write a little something in my diary and say a quiet little prayer before sleep. I would write, "Mum's in a funny mood. Again!" A lot of my feelings were tied up with my relationship with my mum. It was very strained. The diaries are no longer difficult to read, they are more a reminder of how far I have come, a reminder that I am no longer that wounded, needy child.

Mum would tell me that she'd spent time with her father, that he had given her gifts or told her he loved her. On the outside, wearing my mask, I would lie and tell her I was pleased for her but on the inside, I was screaming, "You're choosing him over me!" Mum's keeping in touch with her father provided me with more false lies that I wasn't worthy and didn't matter.

I was utterly confused. Why was Mum trying to hold on to a relationship that caused her so much heartache? Today I understand but at the time I interpreted it as her choosing him over me. It is a normal, innate need for children to crave a deep connection with their parents, even when we are adults. Mum had not cut the cord that kept her attached to her father. In fact, I had not cut the cord either. In a way I was still attached to him. I believed I owed him forgiveness. I thought I wasn't allowed to be angry with him and when I did feel angry, I felt guilt for that.

I believed it was my responsibility to reassure him, "I forgive you. Please don't feel bad for what you did to me. I still love you. Really." I never said those words, but my learned behaviour indicated them. I was behaving towards DC how my mum was. This is only natural I suppose since she was the adult and I was the child, but of course so many adults are still childlike in their relationship with their parents. Mum was seeking an emotional attachment with DC, I was seeking one with her, and we were unable to find it with each other whilst still remaining connected to him.

In later years the cord that kept me attached to DC changed and I was attached to him by my anger, hatred and resentment, wondering who I might have been if he hadn't abused me. This was only harming me, not him. Unaware bitterness was keeping the wound open.

Healing was able to take place once I cut that cord, once I began to discover my own self-worth and identity. It was then that I realised he didn't matter to me. I wanted to focus on my future, my choices, my needs because I finally mattered. Thinking about him and what he did was a waste of my time and energy. I chose to embrace a better life and to reach my full potential. I was only hurting myself, holding myself back.

I needed to work through all the layers, processing that I was allowed to be angry at DC, at my mum and both parents for a time. It was empowering to have and own and explore those feelings with the help of my therapist. It was this empowerment that eventually led to me reporting DC and the sexual abuse. My thoughts on the day I called the police were, Enough is enough. It is NOT my fault. He can now face and own the blame and shame. I am giving it back to him.

This was a turning point for my parents too. Until then, I didn't feel I was receiving the loyalty I needed from my mum. I have been able to speak truthfully with Mum and she has been able to tell me that she is truly sorry.

When I was in hospital, I wrote this letter to Paul's parents.

Dear Mum and Dad,

I've got plenty of time to think in here, I think about what you mean to me and why.

Firstly, you accepted and welcomed me into your family. I was only 16 and it was one of my first experiences of being liked outside of my own family. Well, my Dad likes me anyway. Mum does love me but when I lived at home, Mum and I didn't get on.

The last two years have been a roller coaster for me, and you have been there for me all the way. You have been generous with your love, supporting me when I felt low and weak.

You have helped Paul and me practically with the children etc.

Without reward or recognition.

So what I'm trying to say is, I love you very much. I'm shy and that's why I have written it all down. You really are like parents to me. You are role models and I hope Paul and I can be like you towards Luke and Amelia.

All my love

Amf x

As I read the letter again, I cannot help but notice how childlike I sound, wondering how old I felt when putting pen to paper. The letter highlights the frictions that Mum and I experienced growing up and frictions that had not yet been explored. When I was in hospital, she wrote the following letter.

My Darling Amf,

It's my turn to write to you now. I've been loath to do it thus far because I refuse to accept this condition of yours as a permanent thing. I had felt that by doing the thing that you wanted, I would be accepting your illness and I don't want to do that. But this morning as I sat down to write out that reading for you, I thought if this is going to encourage you at this time then I will do it.

Amf, you have always been such a blessing to me, even from the time you were born. I remember when I fell pregnant with you, how elated I was, and as my tummy began to grow was just so proud of being pregnant with my first baby. And unlike the other 2 pregnancies, I felt so well. I could have jumped to the moon and back carrying you, I just wanted to show off to everyone. So you see, Amf, right from the start there was something special.

As a baby you were an absolute angel. You were an idyllic child. You only ever cried if you were poorly or in pain. You slept right through the night from just a few days old. Even as a young toddler you were lovely. I had loads of cuddles with you – you were a bit of a (wiggly) worm though. At school you never caused us any problems (even though Miss Weeks did call you a dreamboat, but you did take after your dad, eh!). You always worked hard, you were never top of the class or anything, but always had an excellent report. I never asked any more of you than that you would do your best and you always did.

As you entered the teenage years there were never any real problems with you. We had the usual boyfriend heartaches, the trying of different hairstyles, experimenting with fashion. Loud music was never an issue. I will always remember you playing the Bangles song over and over and over again. Compared to today's rubbish we were blessed I reckon. I know that as you reached the middle teen years we went through a period of time where we clashed, but I can now see that this was because we were so much alike. You, like me weren't really into following the crowd. You weren't afraid to be your own person. You were a homely girl as I was.

You always maintained your walk with God at all times, and there were some difficult times for you at school too. Like your dad and me, you were bullied, but it still did not deter your walk with God, or stop you being the person you were. I was always proud of you for that. I know you tried a few discos, nightclubs etc (which you were honest enough to tell us about at a later date), but you made the decision to leave that stuff behind for a more separate walk with God. You listened to your heart. You have always known what is right and holy and what isn't. That is why you have grown to be the lovely person that you are.

As you got through those mid-teen years, I could see this beautiful young women developing. You were pretty, had a figure to die for, a mature character, compassionate and thoughtful ways. You were a daughter that I could be proud of. You were showing an interest in helping others with your work at St. Bartholomew's School. This is a lovely quality that you still have. Often putting others before yourself. Nothing is ever too much trouble. Perhaps too much, eh! I think that one lesson you must learn now is to say no at times.

As your sisters and brother started finding their feet and going off into the world, you were the one that supported Dad and me. When I looked to me as a Mum that my child rearing days had been a total waste of time, you were the one that encouraged and prayed for me. I would only have to look at your life and what God was doing in you, and I would be encouraged that God was with me. I would look at them and know that you had had the same discipline but had made your choice not to go the same way as them. I believe this is because every day I used to pray for all my children that God would keep you all, and that you would all serve him. I still have a plaque on the wall that says, "As for me and my house, we will serve the Lord" and I have underlined the word will. (Joshua 24:15). I believe that God has had His hand on you, Amf, right from the beginning. (Jeremiah 1:5). The fact that you ended up with a Christian husband, and have been blessed financially, must be a witness to the others.

I believe that when you come through this, and you will, I believe that you are going to be mightily used of God. "For I can do all things through Christ who strengthens me". (Philippians 4:13). "Greater is He who is in us than he that is in the world". (1 John 4:4) Remember, Amf, God's word is "sharper than a 2 edged sword". (Hebrews 4:12). It is the greatest weapon we have against the powers of Satan.

I want you to know that I love you loads, I'm proud of the way you've grown up. Keep that lovely humble spirit that you have before God. You are going to be fine and greatly used. You are special, you are the apple of God's eye. Remember that old poem of mine, I'm only a common housewife. At the time I wrote it, I wanted to get the message across that we don't have to be anybody big or famous, just be ourselves.

Just be you, Amf. The person God made you to be.

Lots and lots and lots of love. Mummy.

In March 2016, Mum and I finally had a six-hour heart to heart, with our walls down, where we explored and broke down piece by piece what our relationship had been like and the many reasons why.

In contrast to my own mother, my mum-in-law, from the very beginning, would sit and listen as I gabbled on, comforting my tears with gentle words and hugs. My father-in-law is a man of integrity and has a quiet inner strength. Neither of them boast or brag, well, only about their children and grandchildren of course! But in my opinion, that's how it should be. Paul and I have also tried to shower our children with unconditional love.

I feel that like most parents do, we learned from our parents, both from their mistakes and what they got right. We make new mistakes of course, but we also got lots right too.

Dad and I were able to connect on a deeper level than Mum and I did. We had many heart to hearts on long walks and drives, or early mornings before I went to school or work. In later years I would tell my husband Paul, "I am close to Dad and some children don't even have that. I can't complain. I should be grateful." In reality I was just glossing over the loss of attachment that I was feeling, in not having the relationship with my mum that I had craved. But thanks to therapy, Mum's humility and her willingness to listen, I have her, and she has me, the real me.

CHAPTER SEVEN

Childhood Sexual Abuse, religiosity, repetitious praying of the sinner's prayer, combined with toxic shame, were a catalyst for my breakdown.

I credit my therapy, my own hard work, my counselling training, my family and my faith in God for my recovery but I do acknowledge that there are some teachings in the church which, combined with the abuse, were a catalyst for my breakdown.

In my younger years, I would go to church twice every Sunday, and during the morning service and once each month in the evening, I would take communion. Before communion I would pray the sinner's prayer. I asked for all my wrongs to be removed, to be forgiven. For a victim of abuse who is already feeling dirty, holding guilt and shame, owning what has happened, this was devastating and compounded my sense of worthlessness. I never felt worthy of God's love, grace and forgiveness when taking communion. It only added to my guilt and inner dialogue of, "I shouldn't be taking this if I don't believe his gift of grace and forgiveness is for me." I took it anyway to disguise my shame and guilt from others, who would inevitably ask, "I noticed you didn't take communion, are you okay?"

My insecurities were clearly visible, and I had many lovely church leaders and friends in my life who would try to reassure me. "God loves you, He created you for a purpose, you are meant to be here," they would tell me. "He has plans for you and with Him you are able to do all things you put your mind to." I couldn't believe that God valued me so much, that I was his world, that even if I was the only living human, He would still have made that sacrifice to suffer and die. DC's intentions toward me, his abusive affections and the distorted view of what love was, caused me, for a time, to fear and doubt my heavenly Father's love.

"We are all equal in God's sight," I would hear. Er no, I thought. I will never be as good, as Holy, as these spirit-filled Christian church members. I would cry so often in church, or in my own quiet moments with God. I felt clothed in metaphorical dirty rags and confused. I wondered if I was crying because I felt so inferior to those around me or if it was because no one could see my pain and loneliness. What is this constant pain and hurt I am feeling? I would ask myself. I felt pathetic and pitiful.

I instinctively knew to keep quiet about the abuse because it felt wrong. Feeling and owning the shame hindered me in forming lasting, significant friendships as a child.

Shame was not just a feeling but more a belief about who I was. As a consequence, I struggled to make eye contact with most individuals. Pastor noticed this once and asked why I often looked away. The answer (which I did not share with him) was that I looked away because he was my pastor, and I was scared he would see the dirt, filth and shame. If he saw the filth and shame, I believed he would no longer care, he too would reject me. How untrue this was.

The teachings at church were of their time and hell was mentioned a great deal. Most people seemed able to deal with that but for me, it felt too threatening. I believed I was bad, the shame I owned continued to reject God's love. My shame found it easy to listen to: "we are all sinners, we all fall short of God's love, the wage of sin is death". I would hear other words like love, acceptance and forgiveness but those words did not fit my narrative. DC had not only crushed my innocence he had crushed my spirit. I loved going to church, I craved it, God felt like a tangible presence there. In Christianity, there is the concept of the unpardonable sin, which is denouncing God, disbelieving, and denying his existence. I never did this, but the idea of an unpardonable sin played right into my frame of mind, and I became convinced that this was what I had done.

Satan was also a huge presence in my mind. We were taught that he is ever-present, trying to bring believers down but by the choices we make and the way we live, we move closer to God and further away from him. I believed that I was going to hell. I know how far-fetched it all can sound to someone who hasn't been raised in a Christian environment, but the point is that Satan was always a figure I was aware of. Although not my belief now, I once saw Satan as an enemy who was behind every evil act in this world. I remember a church member once explaining, "Satan is why you are suffering, you're under attack." And I was suffering.

From such a happy start at primary school, which quickly went downhill when the abuse began, secondary school was a nightmare. I was withdrawn and vulnerable and became a victim of bullying. I grew tired of fighting for acceptance and would often try to find hiding places at school to avoid wearing the mask of, "I am okay" smiles. I tried to laugh it off with a strength which had long since left me. My education suffered hugely. Why am I no longer achieving at school when the teachers said I had potential? I wondered. I was achieving before, why not now? What's changed? Each parents' evening, I was filled with dread, not because I had been a naughty child, I wasn't, but because the teachers wanted me to interact more.

My poor grades never bothered Mum and Dad. They knew I was a good girl and that was all that mattered to them. "Do your best, God will do the rest." That was a very popular saying at home. One of Dad's diary entries from when I was 12 and had just started secondary school, notes that he and I had just been out on a walk and that I was feeling sad, had no friends at school and was finding schoolwork difficult. The abuse had just stopped at this time. Dad wrote, "I'm at a loss. My 12 year old is feeling all of these things and it's not normal."

A few years later, my teachers advised that I didn't take my GCSEs as failing them would only knock my confidence further. They meant well but their advice confirmed to me that I was a low achiever and I remember feeling like a total failure and crying my eyes out. My parents tried to comfort me, but I didn't believe them when they said that knowing I tried my best was enough for them. I remember thinking that no one would ever take me seriously and that I was, and would only ever be, pitied.

We had a careers adviser at school. Since I had completely lost my sense of identity, I had no idea what I wanted to do, so he recommended I go to college to do a Youth Training Scheme in childcare. I loved children so I was pleased about this, the bonus being that I thought that when I left school the bullying would stop. Not so. Incredibly someone from school got onto the same YTS scheme as me and the bullying continued on the train to and from college, confirming my belief that there was something actually wrong with me. I was really scared. Then the tutor said that if there was any bullying we should speak up. I plucked up the courage to tell her, and it ended.

As part of our studies we went on placements and on one of mine I met a lady called Jill who sensed my vulnerability and took me under her wing. She was so supportive and kind. Her stepson married my sister, so we met again years later, and she confirmed to me that she had sensed that something had happened to me, and I confirmed to her that I had been abused.

After college, I worked at a special needs school, then a textiles factory. Most of our clothes were for Marks & Spencer and I really enjoyed that job, mainly because the people who worked there didn't seem to judge me. I wanted to better myself, so I soon left and went to Thanet College where I studied various things including welfare in society and home nursing. This effort was indicative of my inner struggle and turmoil and, I believe, of the real me fighting with the damaged part of me. There were so many people around me, particularly at church, who loved me and valued me. I received endless encouragement, but it was always dragged down by my shattered confidence.

I fought hard to finish my first year at Thanet College and was proud to get one GCSE at grade C and two D grades. At least I passed the two Ds, I told myself. They weren't U for ungraded! But then I left college as I didn't feel I could muster enough self-belief to complete the course. This wasn't a one-off. Many projects were started and never finished because I had no confidence to see them through.

I felt crushed but also that perhaps I would be able to do something with my life. I started working at the church playgroup and stayed there for nine years, eventually doing an NVQ level three in childcare. Even then, though, I couldn't take the credit for that as Paul had typed up my coursework for me. I felt that all my research and written work was discredited because I couldn't use the computer.

I constantly hit the self-destruct button. People around me tried to help but believing their intentions was so difficult. My NATs told me I was unlovable, ugly, dirty, undesirable, a horrible person and that no one wanted to be my friend, that the time they gave me came from a place of pity.

"Anthea, you're so sweet and lovely," people would tell me. "You're kind and a great listener. You're caring, clever, discerning and gifted, loved and special."

I told myself these were nothing but lies, people felt obliged to tell me these things. To believe those truths was far too scary and would have taken me out of my harmful comfort zone, my false sense of security. I needed my familiar world, or so I thought. To entertain the thought that I was more, I could be more, achieve more and mean more to others was far too overwhelming. It was safer to believe that I was nothing and meant nothing.

CHAPTER EIGHT

When I was 15, I joined the church youth group. We would go laser-gunning, swimming and to the cinema. Even though you could join from the age of 15, the other members of the youth group were much older than me and I don't think some were particularly happy that I had joined. Years later I discovered that whilst in my mid to late teens, those slightly older individuals who seemingly took me under their wing and befriended me, were actually laughing about me behind my back. This hurt and also confirmed my NATs: I'm pathetic. My purpose is to be laughed at.

Paul was a member of the church youth group and even though he was 18, he was very shy. I had spotted Paul at church and had liked him from the moment I saw him. He was quiet, mysterious and really good looking. He had all this black hair which he wore in a flat-top and I loved the way he dressed in his own unique style of jeans with roll-ups and brown suede shoes. I had been praying for a nice, Christian boyfriend, convinced that the odds were against me not only because there weren't many eligible boys at church but also because I didn't think anyone would look at me twice.

Sunday nights at church became all about Paul. I was convinced he was the answer to my prayers, but prayers weren't all that was required here. Nope! It was going to take a perm to win the man of my dreams! Mousse, a diffuser – the 80s version of straighteners which made your hair massive rather than sleek – they were my tools, and I went for it. I would later find out that Paul didn't care for this massive hair and that I only caught his attention when I went from the perm to the Princess Diana which was less mousse but a whole can of hairspray.

When I joined the youth group, I would sneak the occasional look at Paul and when he caught me, he would look away quickly. There was a wedding we both attended. Paul remembers my navy blue dress – Princess Diana's influence here cannot be overestimated! But he loved that dress and within a couple of weeks, some of the other youth group members, our mutual friend Maria and some helpers, realised what was going on and did a bit of match-making. They shoved us into the kitchen together to make the drinks and Paul, not quite the romantic, spluttered: "So, I think we should make a go of it."

For some reason, most likely shock and fear, I told him I would think about it! What was I thinking? But a couple of days later I gave him my answer and the universe and the ozone layer (you have to be an 80s kid to get this reference) breathed a sigh of relief.

It wasn't all plain-sailing. I was very insecure in the relationship, always thinking that Paul was looking at someone else, that he pitied me or could find someone better. I had him on a pedestal, which he didn't like. I couldn't accept that he had chosen me. I asked Paul recently who I was when he met me and who he fell in love with. It's interesting to me because with the sense of self that I have now, I can look back and see how many masks I was wearing then. He says I was sweet, loving, caring, ditsy. He even liked how awkwardly I ran when we played rounders. Isn't that lovely? I couldn't relax enough to appreciate this at the time though, so even though I enjoyed our dates to the Beefeater or times spent with our parents or a walk on the beach where we would sneak a kiss, it was tinged with my insecurities.

In this year, I wrote in my diary: March 13, 1990. "Went to church feeling terrible. Also went for a long walk at the beach on my own, I have the POMS – Poor Old Me Thoughts. It is all to do with the deep personal, own problem (a reference to DC). And to make things worse, we were visited by the police to be told Nan has died but went peacefully in her sleep. Oh God, I loved her so much."

Nine days later, I went to see Nan Fox in the Chapel of Rest and wrote: Really miss Nan, used to be able to talk to her about anything. Went to see Mum no.2 (Paul's Mum) she gave me a lovely hug and cried with me, I love her!

The impact of Nan's Fox's death didn't hit me as much as it might have if I hadn't already been depressed at the time. I was given her beautiful pink teddy bear as a keepsake.

Paul was very focused on his faith with God. It was something we enjoyed together although I was slightly put out when he went on a local church event on the day of my 18th birthday. Paul says he regrets that to this day. Mum's parents were there though. It's not an 18th birthday that I want to remember.

It was around this time that I decided to tell Paul about the abuse. I spoke to my dad and pastor first and they agreed that it was a good idea and that I should do it in case Paul found out later and thought I didn't trust him. For me, I knew that I had a secret and that Paul and I didn't have secrets.

I diarised my feelings about it in May, writing: I don't know what's up with me lately? I seem to be in the blues a lot of the time. I wish I could snap out of it. I keep thinking about Nan Fox, then there's 'the usual' about Grandad C still. I would like to tell Paul, but every time there seems an opportunity, the words just don't come out. With me being like this I'm scared Paul will get fed up with me and not put up with the way I am anymore. I hate having ups and downs as frequently as I do, it shouldn't be like this.

Paul and I were out for a walk when I told him. I didn't say much, only that my grandfather had done something not very nice to me when I was younger. I could see that Paul knew what I meant but that the seriousness of it didn't really sink in. I know that he had never heard of sexual abuse or anything like it at the time.

At around the same time, Dad wrote in his diary: Anthea feels a black cloud hanging over her. (She) feels guilty as she didn't try to stop him. How can a child be expected to do anything about advances from their grandfather? Tries to tell herself it was a dream or didn't really happen as he denied it all! Feels dirty. Already interfering with an otherwise happy relationship with her boyfriend. Paul commented (to me), "She has a happy, smiling face but sad eyes." This whole issue bugs her quite often.

By this time Paul was 21 and working for the bank which he'd done since school. There wasn't a proposal as such. I went to visit him, and he said, "I'm going to marry you one day." I floated off to church music practice like I was on a cloud.

I was 20 when we married on August 1, 1992. Our pastor married us. In 2017 he also conducted the ceremony to celebrate our silver wedding anniversary of 25 years, which meant so much to us. Despite DC being in attendance, our wedding day was happy. I was married at 20 and broke down at 30 and for those 10 years, I think you could say I was on autopilot. It was a perfectly structured life. We had two children, Luke born in April 1995 and Millie born January 1998. Within our own little bubble I was ecstatically happy. But the smiles, the laughs, were not a reflection of what I was feeling on the inside. I had everything that anybody could wish for but inside I was broken, and I spent almost all of my energy papering over the cracks. People on the outside – the odd few I did open up to – said that it looked like I had it all: the husband, two lovely children, a home, a job, the car, holidays. Some couldn't understand why I was sad.

Paul knew that I wasn't right. Some evenings we would have our own prayer times together. I would talk and cry, normally triggered by something had been said in church, something that had been preached about, something that had triggered a hurt.

I would also talk to Paul and Dad about a feeling that I had that I didn't know who I was. "I've got no purpose," I would tell them. "What am I doing here? I have no idea; I am just existing" I didn't keep a journal around that time as I was busy with the family and working part-time at the playgroup with Mum, but I was still depressed. It was always a struggle to get up in the mornings. I would dread the phone going and I would sometimes hide if there was a knock at the door, even if it was a casual visit from a family member or friend. I was emotionally and mentally exhausted and wanted to hide. The many masks I was wearing became exhausting and confusing. I got to a point where I didn't know which mask to wear for who. I felt like a complete fake and was so scared that someone would figure me out.

I pushed on, ever the people pleaser, doing what made others happy and rarely going against their wishes. I did not want to be the cause of others' discontentment. If they wanted to go to the park but I wanted to go to the beach, we would go to the park. If I was booking dinner for 7pm but they wanted to meet at 6pm, I changed the time. I rarely felt empowered to share my needs or preferred choices. I did not want others to feel put out or guilty because of me. My own responsibilities would be put on hold, even if I knew it meant running around like a headless chicken after I had spent time helping someone. My frame of reference was: If I say yes, if I do this, I will be valued, loved, accepted, liked. Actually there is less respect given to people pleasers but for me to hear that people thought I would do whatever was asked was where I was comfortable. A brief moment of appreciation kept me going.

Because I wasn't sure of myself, I did seem to get a lot of advice from people. I'm sure a lot of what was said could be dismissed as banter – there was a sense that I was ditsy – but I didn't like it. I would laugh at my own expense. I was desperate to prove myself and the people that sensed that, tried to motivate and encourage me, but it hurt. I began to notice specific frustrations in the people around me. I wanted to shout that I could do it and I didn't need to be told or parented but I couldn't verbalise it. I became sulky, passive aggressive, sarcastic. I didn't know who I was so how could I expect others to know who I was?

CHAPTER NINE

The young man walked towards us. I wouldn't have noticed him except that it was a bright June day, and he was looming in front of me dressed head-to-foot in black. Even his shoulder-length, curly hair was black. A goth, I wondered. I tried to look away but then I noticed his t-shirt. What the…? My stomach lurched. I shuddered and looked away, then back again. I stared at the image; the vile words written in white lettering on the black background. It didn't say what I thought it said, did it? The words reached for me like talons. I felt myself being pulled towards them, a blanket of hell encircling me.

Hail Satan. Fuck God

The words sliced through me. It was me they were talking to. I was the one. I had renounced God. I had committed the unpardonable sin. My life was honouring Satan not God and I was bound for hell. The man swept past. He was gone but the words were burned into my mind. My world spun on its axis, and I knew that everything I thought about myself was true. I owned that t-shirt, its design, its words. It was me who had spewed those disgusting words into the world.

It had been a normal morning up until that point. Just the average stresses of motherhood. Luke has ADHD, which was undiagnosed at that point, so I'd spent the morning getting him to concentrate on eating his breakfast and stop playing long enough to clean his teeth, get dressed, tie his shoes and pick up his bag. It was hard going but once I got him ready and put Millie in the buggy, we were a happy trio. Until I saw that t-shirt.

I dropped Luke at school and pushed Millie home again. The words Hail Satan, Fuck God were all I could think about. They swam in front of my eyes, between me and the house, my coffee cup, between me and Millie, between me and reality. Why can't I get it out of my mind? Why am I a bad person? Why am I still thinking about this? I told no one what I'd seen and over the next eight weeks, the harder I fought to rid myself of those words, the more regular and more intense they became. I watched television and listened to music in an attempt to drown out the words but that only worked temporarily.

I was suffering from acute OCT or Obsessive Compulsive Thoughts, one of the ways in which Obsessive Compulsive Disorder manifests. My mental health was declining rapidly. I had developed anorexia earlier that year, getting thinner and thinner until by my birthday in May; I weighed just six and a half stone. I wanted to die, and I thought the easiest way would be to stop eating. I hated myself so much that I even berated myself for choosing to die that way, since it seemed painless and cowardly. Later that same month I had attended a friend's hen weekend and at the end of the night when Paul drove me back to the hotel, I burst into tears in the car park. Paul asked what was wrong. I didn't know.

OCD is not just checking locks, light switches, washing hands and cleaning the toilet 50 times a day. It can also manifest the way it did for me. OCT can be fairly common for Christians or people of any faith but when we are well, we enjoy the rhythms of our faith. Within eight weeks the thoughts filled my every waking second and sleep was barely any respite as although I wanted to sleep to escape, I was petrified that the thoughts would be there when I woke up. I barely spoke. I stopped functioning. I couldn't look after the house, Paul or the children.

Millie had the most gorgeous, long hair in ringlets. When I was a young teenager, Mum had cut my hair because she said I wasn't looking after it. In hindsight I can see this was due to the depression I was suffering but it made me adamant that Millie would have long, beautiful hair if that was what she wanted. I usually loved styling it in French plaits and ponytails but after the t-shirt, I stopped. I wasn't doing my own hair either or applying make-up. I wore baggy trousers and a tracksuit top. I didn't wash or clean my teeth. All my energy went towards trying to rid my mind of these images and thoughts. I was locked inside my mind. We moved in with Paul's parents so that they could care for the children. I withdrew.

Hail Satan. Fuck God. I was in that bedroom alone. I was completely isolated. Life was going on around me, but it was muffled. But the thoughts, they were deafening.

Hail Satan. Fuck God. The solution was clear. I needed to go to sleep and not wake up.

Hail Satan. Fuck God. I moved towards the window.

Me as a toddler, before the abuse began

Aged 12 years, after the abuse had just ended. The effects are clear; I can see a great sadness in my eyes

Millie and me, where I am in the grip of anorexia in the lead up to my breakdown

But better days were ahead, and here I am having fun, riding the Burnham Bends, Burnham-on-Crouch, Essex, on my Triumph Tiger 900 GT PRO

Paul and I, this first picture of us doing what we love most — spending time with our motorcycle buddies. It was taken by our photographer friend Ryan Stevens (www.itsjustusphotography.co.uk)

CHAPTER TEN

"Well, I was abused by my grandad. But it was just an act. A physical act." I said this in a tone of voice that indicated that this couldn't possibly have anything to do with the fact that I was severely mentally ill. I was in a consultation with my doctor and my psychiatrist, and they were trying to discover what had caused my breakdown. I talked about a serious car accident we'd had the previous year. I mentioned that I'd recently been a little stressed about my best friend's wedding cake that I'd made and safely transported to its destination, a four-hour drive away from home and that we had also moved house.

"But there must be something else. Trauma in your childhood? Did something happen to you?"

And that was when I said it. It hadn't even crossed my mind. How amazing to be that naïve. Of course for the professionals, that was it, they had their answer, they had something to work with.

My early days in hospital were upsetting but I also felt relieved that I might be getting some help. Being on my own the first night was frightening. I was in a room on my own, door kept open, by the nurse's station so I could be closely monitored. I felt very alone. I was assessed, filling in multiple choice questionnaires. I ticked boxes that explained I felt: "Sad all the time and can't snap out of it, that I have nothing to look forward to, I feel guilty and punished constantly, unable to cry even though I want to; I feel tired, ugly, much less interested in sex and that I want to kill myself."

I was prescribed Fluoxetine, used to treat depression or obsessive compulsive disorder; Olanzapine, an antipsychotic that treats mania and Carbamazepine to stabilise moods. Of course the biggest symptom of my illness was shame and the repeated, unwanted images about the t-shirt, which were what was driving me to want to kill myself, but no one knew that.

I stayed at Medway Maritime for just over a month and then I was discharged. I didn't want to stay and since I had gone into hospital voluntarily and not been sectioned, I was free to leave. I left on a Friday and Paul and I took our children home but on the Saturday night, Paul found me trying to cut my wrists with a bread knife. That wasn't an attempt on my life. Cutting my wrists gave me a few seconds relief from the thoughts. I didn't want to die, I wanted to get out of my head and into my body for a moment.

Paul was furious. Not with me but because he felt I had been discharged to free up a bed. Clearly, I wasn't ready to go home and the next day I went back to hospital but since there wasn't a bed at Medway, I was sent to Dartford, which on top of everything else was a much more difficult journey for everyone who wanted to visit me.

I stayed there while the medics waited for a bed to come up at Medway. While I was in Dartford, I tried to hang myself and it was then that I opened up about the thoughts and how frequent they were. The doctors realised that they needed to focus on the Obsessive Compulsive Thoughts before anything else as they could clearly see that the reason I was trying to take my own life was because I was trying to escape the thoughts.

I know now that it's best to admit to Obsessive Compulsive Thoughts. You need to tell someone you trust what's going on in your mind so that you're not owning the shame. But at the time, I believed I should be able to control the thoughts. All this did was increase my anxiety about them and intensify and magnify them. Of course my mind was ready to crash and if it hadn't been the t-shirt, it would have been something else to trigger the breakdown. I was prescribed electroconvulsive therapy, known as ECT. This is a process that sees electric currents sent through the brain to trigger an epileptic seizure. It's had some pretty bad press in the past; it was often considered brutal and administered without anaesthetic and sometimes without consent or as punishment. It was featured in the 70s film One Flew Over The Cuckoo's Nest when patients on a mental ward are sent to the Shock Shop to stop them rebelling.

ECT is still an intense treatment, something of a last resort used to treat life-threatening depression, but I knew only what I was told, which sounded very positive. I would be given the treatment under general anaesthetic and given a muscle relaxant so that I wouldn't convulse. The doctors explained to me that ECT would "re-set my brain" by altering my brain chemistry and that when I came back onto the ward, I probably wouldn't remember the thoughts or the treatment. ECT does have some side effects, most notably memory loss – usually short-term – similar to what people with epilepsy suffer.

Despite this, I was relieved when I was told, and I actually couldn't wait. I was told that the thoughts might return but that I would be given tools like Cognitive Behavioural Therapy (CBT) to manage them so that by the time they did come, I would be ahead and have some methods of coping with them.

I don't remember anything about the treatment apart from being wheeled to the room in which it was administered and then waking up on the ward. There was an immediate improvement and a huge gap in my thoughts where the images had been. I knew that I had previously had obsessive thoughts, but I had no clue what they were. I cannot tell you how amazing that was! For the first time in many, many months I felt that there was hope.

My care plan in October stated that I needed to reduce the frequency and severity of intrusive thoughts, reduce my generalised anxiety and self-report thoughts and distress. I was still extremely unwell. My sister Sue recalls coming to see me and taking me out to Capstone Park. She says I was a tiny, childlike being, gripping hold of the pink teddy bear that had been Nan Fox's and rocking in my chair. Clearly, I was trying to comfort my inner child.

Luke and Millie were eventually able to visit me, and I was filled with joy as I saw them enter the ward. I couldn't wait to hold them and ask them their news. I missed them constantly, which caused me to cry many times. I felt angry with myself, hating missing out on what they were getting up to, and I felt sad when I heard from my father-in-law that Luke had been bullied and that he had stepped in. I was filled with shame, as I knew I should have been the one to support Luke. I called mum-in-law to ask how my children were and cried telling her that I missed them, overwhelmed by guilt. She was lovely, reassuring me they were okay and telling me to concentrate on getting well so I could come home. As a family we could have not pulled through without them stepping in to take constant care of our children.

The goal was for my OCT to be reduced by half by November 6. I was to be given a notebook in which to write down the incidents of my OCT in a 24-hour period. I was to respond to therapeutic interventions by attending at least three activities with occupational therapy, which were beauty treatments, arts and crafts and relaxation classes. I was to be encouraged to attend relaxation groups and formal time was to be offered to me twice a week in which I could discuss my anxieties and issues that may be linked to my OCT. The professionals in the hospital were very mindful of the vulnerable situation I was in and knew that I wasn't ready to look at the abuse.

CHAPTER ELEVEN

I kept a diary in hospital and have included the following extracts to show my state of mind:

> Monday, November 4: I want to thank you Lord for my family and thank you that all my needs are provided. I want to thank you Lord, even though I'm waiting for a complete healing, I am on the mend now. Jesus, I want to live a life that pleases You. Jesus I've been saying 'I want my life back' but what I really mean is I desire a new life in You, a new way of living. My aim is to please You, Serve You.
>
> Tuesday, November 5: Oh Lord be with me always, be by my side. Thank you for the knowledge you gave the doctors concerning ECT and for the way it has helped me. The thoughts have gone, and I feel so, so free.
>
> Thank you, for answered prayer, thank you for moving and working in my life.
>
> Thursday, November 7: Is this what 'being in the battle' is all about? I hate it! I will NOT turn my back on You Lord Jesus. These intrusive thoughts are not of You, and they are not me either. I love you Jesus and I want to serve You. Please Jesus remove ALL the bad thoughts so I can serve You. I promise you will be number one in my life when you free me from this hell, that's how much I want to be free Jesus. I promise that my main aim will be to serve you Father. (My prayers growing up were the same, 'I desire to serve you full time Jesus'.) I'm sorry Lord that it has not been that way up till now. Please forgive me Lord. Please Lord may I wake one morning and know that you have healed me, knowing You've worked a miracle in my life. May Your answer come quickly.

It is important to note here that I believed I could earn healing by serving God. I was trying to convince Him that I was useless, broken but too naïve to realise that what I was in fact asking was "I'm bad God, can I redeem myself and receive healing if I'm a good person from now on?"

> Friday, November 8: Dear Lord please call me, I want to know that I am serving You. I need to know that I am serving You. I need to know that I am fulfilling Your will in my life, I don't want to feel that I am wasting time anymore. (I am giving God all the reasons why I 'think' he needs to heal me – funny!) I'm 30 years of age and time goes so fast Lord; I want to know I am walking in your footsteps. I don't want to be doing my own thing, meaninglessly filling in my time. May I know beyond a shadow of a doubt that You have spoken to me so I can do Your will and be happy doing Your will. Lord please hear my cry; my heart is for You. Please heal my mind so it can be wholly for You also. Please fill me with Your peace, Lord, I do trust You, I know that plenty of prayer has been offered up to You, so everything is in Your hands, You are in control. Please, please cleanse me Lord, I pray, please cleanse me a sinner, I'm so, so unworthy of Your blood. Please wash me clean. Thank you for the work You have done so far.

Reading this today, in 2021, I can see why some may feel my faith was a hindrance more than a support. It may come across that because I believed I was unworthy, that I was beyond redemption, beyond saving and healing, this only made my mental state worse. I heard and believed from church teachings only what was easy for me to hear and believe. I felt like a lost sinner so that's what I heard and believed. My fears and anxieties prevented me from hearing what the teaching of my faith were really saying, "His grace makes us worthy; His forgiveness sets us free, gives us hope, His love brings healing, joy and peace."

Despite knowing these gifts and blessings were the truth and wanting it for myself – seeing, envying, admiring it in others' lives – I believed that I was dirty and therefore unworthy. I was unable to accept and receive God's forgiveness and find peace and joy and so on. If I did find these things, they were short lived as the effects of the abuse had a foothold in my life and had created my negative core beliefs.

With current insights I now understand that if God had provided the overnight healing I so craved, it could not have been permanent. The dormant, unprocessed, unacknowledged feelings of hate, anger, and resentment would keep me trapped until I dealt with them. I listened to worship music on my headphones and found the lyrics about dark days, feeling lost but finding hope, being raised up, victorious and conquering, very inspiring. I needed to hear uplifting lyrics. I continued to write:

Saturday, November 9: Thank you, Jesus, for my life, thank you that You created me for a reason, for a purpose. You didn't create me for this hell I'm in and going through. Dear Jesus let there be an end to this hell soon, I need my life back. I do thank you Lord for my family, my husband, my children, thank you for giving them to me, they are gifts from You, provisions from You. Oh Jesus You alone are the answer to my needs, I call out to You again and again. What lessons are You trying to teach me? I feel like I'm being punished for something. I'm so sorry Lord if I have done anything wrong, anything that's hurt You. Surely me wanting to end my life means I can't cope anymore. Oh dear Jesus please hear my cry.

Sunday, November 10: Today, I would like to begin by saying thank you for my family, for my husband and my children. Thank you for all the love, Paul has to offer and the great way he looks after his family. Also thank you for the endless ways he tries to look after me. Please bless him. Thank you for all You have provided, I have so much in my life, all my needs are met, this is a grateful heart.

The many thank yous throughout these prayer entries are me trying to focus on my blessings, mainly Paul and the children, giving myself reasons not to end my life. The magnitude of shame, I believed God may have been punishing me.

Tuesday, November 12.: Dear Lord please hear me call on Your name, where are You Lord? Where are You Jesus? Why am I having to suffer so much. I need You so much, I feel so lonely. (My thought process: He must have given up, deserted me because I am a hopeless, helpless, lost cause.) Please forgive me, completely wash me clean, wash me in Your blood, purify my heart, wash me in the blood of the lamb. I am in such desperate need of You Father; I have no direction to turn. Be in control Father of my mind, complete control, I ask it in Your name. You are my only answer; You are the only one I can lean on. Lord please heal my mind completely. May I find full rest in You.

You can see intense religiosity here. I am still trying to be someone that I am not. A girl who had no idea who she was, using religious language I'd heard growing up, not quite the thees, thys and therefores but close. When I read my diaries back, I hear a lost soul who was oppressed as well as depressed. Now I know He has given us what we need, the answers, the know-how; the strength was within me already, as well as believing in God, I needed to believe in 'me' as He does.

I was in a storm, Jesus was saying, step out of the boat walk towards me, towards healing, but I was too afraid. I believed I would sink, even though, deep down I knew God would meet me halfway if I took that leap of faith and climbed out of the boat. Yes, we do thank God for being so good, but He also wants us to see ourselves as He sees us. Made for victory not brokenness. Deep down I knew God was cheering me on to achieve, free will is a wonderful thing, He was never going to drag me out of the boat kicking and screaming. This was never going to be a magic wand experience; it has been working through the many painful layers that has empowered me and made me stronger.

Thursday, November 14: [*My words here sound contradictory, evidence of the state of confusion I was in*] Thank you for all the blessings in my life, that all my needs are met and more besides. Oh Lord, this is a grateful heart, my life is blessed abundantly, but I feel so unworthy of all these blessings. You are so good to me Lord. I come to You asking for a cleansing, Lord please wash me in Your blood, please, please, wash me in Your blood. Please, please, please purify my heart; I need Your grace and mercy. I am so unworthy of Your love. (Now I pray thank you that your forgiveness, love and mercy has made me worthy of You.)

Oh Father I cry out to You again and again, I need You, where are you. I cannot get through this without Your help Lord. I feel like I'm crying alone through this crisis, please reveal Yourself to me in some way, show me I'm not alone. Please can I have my life back? I want to take my children to school, iron my husband's shirts (today this makes me smile as I no longer want to iron them and I don't!), go to work, take the children to their after school clubs, cook my family their dinner and so on. Oh Jesus why do I feel so alone, Lord God WHERE ARE YOU? Why have You allowed this to happen to me? I have no control over what goes on in my mind. This is too scary for me to bear. Please God work a miracle in my life. Please please please, I cannot do this on my own. Amen and amen.

Friday, November 15: I hate this feeling of wanting to end it, I cannot cope. Only You can deal with this problem, I cannot deal with this alone. Please be in control Father, You alone are the answer, that's why I turn to You again and again. Please Father don't make me pray this prayer anymore. Lord I want to be a winner in You. Please give me complete control.

Wednesday, November 20: Dear Lord Jesus, I come to You this morning asking You for a cleansing; please wash me clean, purify my heart I pray. (I was not dirty; I was owning DC shame. If I had listened, I would have heard God say, You are blameless, don't own your grandfather's guilt, his filth, the shame which is his, not yours.)

Oh Lord I don't understand this but this I do know, You're a loving father who understands, You understand everything. Oh Father I am still in great need, I still need to be set free, I want my, need my, life back, my children, my husband, my home and that all comes with that. I'm missing Luke and Amelia, I'm missing Paul, I need to look after them and our home.

I went home briefly for Christmas in 2002 and then left hospital in 2003. I continued self-harming, again not to end my life but to feel something other than the mental and emotional pain I was in. I was frightened of coping alone. I had felt safe in the hospital, really cocooned, institutionalised I suppose and although I was supported really well by the NHS Crisis Care Team, I was still frightened. I took a couple of overdoses. I think it was the reality of having to face the sexual abuse and the impact and consequences of it.

I got a lot of support from my church. One scripture that the then minister gave me was, "For he has not given us the spirit of fear but of power, love, and a sound mind."

Dad had always told me, "God has many promises in the Bible. When you pray, read them out to him. Remind him: God, You say in your word 'this'. He wants us to claim His promises and healing."

I tried to do this, but it really bothered me that I believed in a healing God but that I was dependant on tablets. I was still so insecure and preoccupied with everyone around me and how much better they were doing. Everyone else was able to function without tablets, why couldn't I? It would take me a long time to realise how much my limited thinking had been programmed by the sexual abuse.

One day I was decorating my daughter's bedroom. I was up the ladder, and the image of the t-shirt came back. I called out, "In the name of Jesus these thoughts will be removed. For God has not given me a spirit of fear but of power, of love and of sound mind!" I felt self-conscious when praying out loud, but I did it anyway. I was determined. I wanted to be well. I had good things. I had a lovely husband, lovely children, a lovely home. I knew there was potential for a good life. And I wanted to enjoy what I had. I was fed up with being frightened all the time. The thoughts went and I felt incredible joy in the realisation that I was going to get well, that I had control, my past experiences no longer controlled me, I had a future, and hope.

People were praying for me, I was praying and hanging on to God's promises even though for a long time I believed I was unworthy of His goodness. It was a tough struggle holding on to my faith when my world had been turned upside down and I was left feeling lost; I was in a confusing maze created by others with no direction or way out. But I clung on, searching for a way out, even those days when I was angry with God. I felt guilty for being angry with God. Dad would say, "Don't worry, it doesn't matter. You're not the first or last person to be angry at God and, actually, God wants us to be real with him."

Loving non-Christian family and friends have asked me why God allowed me to be abused but I believe that God gave us free will and DC abused that freewill for his own selfish gain. Freewill is a gift. We are free to make the choices we make. I used to get so wound up by people saying, "God will turn it in to something good." I thought, "So he's allowing something bad to happen for something good to come of it?" But now I see it as: God does not control us. We are not robots. God is my heavenly, loving father and just as my earthy loving father wants to see me confidently spreading my wings, respecting the gift of free will, so does my heavenly Father. I choose not to abuse this beautiful gift of life. I choose to love and respect others, not abuse and control them.

*

In May 2003, I took an overdose. I was to be in and out of hospital for four years. My father-in-law, together with mum-in-law, was understandably very busy helping to look after Luke and Amelia as well as own individual responsibilities and was unable to visit me often but on one of father-in-law's visits he told me, "Just remember, on Earth, we are just a passing through. One day this will all be over. We're just a passing through. When you look at how long we'll be with God, how long we'll be in Heaven, that's eternity, it will be wonderful, better than we can imagine. We're just passing through."

A passing through. It was a simple thought, a calming one, and it helped me a great deal.

CHAPTER TWELVE

I wouldn't have been able to get well without Paul's support and his incredible ability to love me as I was and to make room in his heart for who I wanted to be and have become. In the months and years that followed my first suicide attempt, Paul kept the family together and was devoted to my care. I thought it was important to share things from his perspective:

> The first thing I noticed about Anthea was that her hair didn't move! I don't think I spoke to her for the first six or seven months of going to church. She seemed very quiet, and I was also shy. I became a Christian in September 1988 and was baptised at the end of the following month. Anthea gave me a card and a music tape to celebrate. The tape was a Christian singer called Amy Grant.
>
> By Christmas of that year, I was starting to really like Anthea. I was nearly 19 and had had one girlfriend but she had approached me, so I had never actually plucked up the courage to ask a girl out. I embarked on a campaign of teasing Anthea, pulling her hairclips out (I noticed her hair stayed in position without them!) and in September 1989 we attended the same wedding. There was country dancing and in one dance, I had to put my hands on Anthea's shoulders. She was wearing a nice long, blue dress.
>
> It was obvious that love was blossoming, and I was getting nagged by my friends. On Wednesday, September 20, 1989, we had music practice at the church. I went off to make drinks and Anthea was sent in to help. I shuffled and stammered until I finally came out with the line I have never been allowed to forget: "Shall we make a go of it?"
>
> It was hardly a line from When Harry Met Sally, the big romantic film of the year and not surprisingly, Anthea made me wait for an answer. Twelve months later, I proposed, and we went to buy a ring. My mum came too to make sure I spent enough. I was known for being tight with money, shall we say!
>
> It was before we were engaged that Anthea told me about the abuse. It was a brief conversation and then nothing more was said. I could see that something was bothering Anthea though. There would be some days in church when she would be quiet and ask someone to pray for her. She didn't feel peaceful or accepted by others. She was

very down on herself and would say to me, "I'm ugly and don't know why you go out with me."

I remember one evening she was kneeling down by the door of my blue Ford Escort saying goodnight and she told me she was ugly. I said, "You're criticising God's work, you know?" I took it on as my mission to try and build her up.

I never connected the abuse with Anthea's behaviour. I was quite naïve and even when she broke down and the doctors asked her what had happened in her life, I never thought that what she'd gone through could have caused her the problems she was suffering. I had never knowingly come across anyone with mental health issues up until that point. I knew she was slowly going, disappearing, if that makes sense? She was losing weight; she would go to bed and then wake up screaming. I would have to shake her out of it. I had to slap her face once. And she was becoming a recluse. She didn't want to go out and meet people, she would sleep a lot during the day. But I am an optimist and I just kept thinking that things would improve.

When Luke was seven and Millie was four and a half, things escalated. I was doing a lot of work on the house so at the weekends, the kids would watch me doing that, while Anthea was in bed. It got to the point where Luke broke up for school holidays and I had to go back to work but I could see that I couldn't leave the children with their mum. That's when we moved in with my parents, on Monday, August 5, 2002.

The previous Friday, my parents were away so I went to their house and spent the whole night praying until 6am. I wanted to be on my own so that I could make some noise and address God as if he was standing in front of me.

On August 8, 2002, four days after we moved in with my parents, Dad rang me to say that Anthea had tried to jump out of the room they'd given us and that I needed to make my way to Medway Maritime Hospital. The sight that greeted me was a very sad Anthea. She wasn't with it, she couldn't speak. She was just sitting there with my dad. Mum was at home with the kids. She was kept in for assessment.

It was a waiting game and a completely bewildering time. I would go to the hospital each day. Even if I worked in London I would come home and go straight there and I made sure I was there for when the doctor came each week to assess Anthea's progress and see if she would be staying in or coming home.

I didn't take the children in at first as I didn't want them to see Anthea the way she was. When I went to visit her, we'd sit and try and talk but I would see this worried look on her face, which was her trying to stop suicidal thoughts. One time, we went for a walk around the hospital grounds and when she got back, she said she'd had thoughts of stepping out in front of the cars. It was shocking to know that she was doing that even when she was with me. She later told me that she was fantasising about it all the time and when she was driving, she would imagine swerving off the road or a bridge.

I don't think I dwelled on the enormity of the situation. I was too busy with visiting Anthea and spending time with the children. At work I had just stepped up to cover a more senior position for a colleague on maternity leave. Everything was happening at once and I didn't have too much time to sit and think. I just ploughed on.

This was to be Anthea's longest spell in hospital, but she was discharged just before Christmas. I don't remember much about the actual day, but I was apprehensive. I didn't know what Anthea would do when I wasn't there. When she had tried to jump out of the window, I had received a call at work. When she tried to hang herself in hospital, I had been called then too. I was nervous but I tried not to mollycoddle her. I tried to manage each day as it came, and I didn't have a sense of the long-term. It didn't cross my mind that she was going to transform and that I was going to get a whole new, strong and confident Anthea!

Anthea continued her treatment through 2003 and in May that year, we took the children to Disneyland Paris. Towards the end of the four-day break, I could see that Anthea was struggling. She was quiet and had a worried look on her face. On the Monday I went to work and planned to get home early to take the kids swimming. When I got home, there was a letter on the dining room table. Anthea was upstairs and she'd taken an overdose. I phoned an ambulance, and she went into hospital for a month. I moved back in with my parents.

That suicide attempt was really distressing for me because the kids were there. I had to ask my parents round to look after them but of course the ambulance turned up while the children were there, and they saw their mum taken away. I felt awful not being able to shield them from it. They were very upset and for years afterwards if Anthea didn't feel well – even if it wasn't to do with mental health – the kids would say, "Mummy's not going back into hospital, is she?"

Anthea spent time in hospital every year up until 2005. In some ways she was her own worst enemy because she would feel well and then, unbeknown to anyone, she would take herself off her medication and would decline again. She did this several times, which prolonged the healing process for Anthea. I knew that she objected to the medication. She was on the maximum doses of very potent drugs from which you need to withdraw slowly, so when she just stopped taking them it was horrendous. But every year the periods in between admissions would get longer. We felt we'd be home and dry if we hit the year mark – a year without admissions, and when we did that, we knew we were on the up.

I know that what happened to Anthea is DC's fault, but I don't like to spend my life dwelling on those things. It's a waste of time as I can't change what's happened. I believe that we can only make the best of where we are now. I'm sure if I saw DC, I would say a few words to him but to be angry with someone and go round to their house and confront them just wasn't me.

I have sometimes wondered what Anthea would be like if the abuse hadn't happened. How would her personality have developed normally? Would she have been totally different? Then I think that what he did wasn't nice but actually, in a perverse sort of way, I should go and thank him because if he hadn't done what he did, Anthea wouldn't be who she is now. She's just fantastic! Confident, strong, loads of self-esteem. It's a funny thought process. She has completely changed, and she is so focused, so driven and resilient. I couldn't be prouder of the woman she is today.

CHAPTER THIRTEEN

"I am just wondering if he deserves that title."

I stared at my therapist. It was three years into my therapy, and I was talking about DC but still calling him Grandad. I was still in the frame of mind that he was my grandfather and I loved him.

"I am just wondering if he deserves that title."

I felt as if someone had switched on a light. Did he deserve that title? Was he a true grandad or was he someone who had done something very wrong and had hurt me? Yes, he was the latter. It hadn't occurred to me that I could take ownership of the situation and my relationship with him and rename it. It was empowering. A good therapist might not say a lot but when they do, it can be life changing. I gave the question a great deal of thought and eventually decided that no, DC did not deserve to be called Grandad. It was the beginning of a new frame of reference for me.

Linda (not her real name) was one of my first psychotherapists. I had her for quite some time, and she was amazing. Linda was very person-centred in her approach and never pushed me or directed the session. She was a great listener. As time progressed, I began the arduous task of unpacking my childhood experiences. Anything I wanted to bring, whatever I was ready to talk about, I talked about with Linda. I needed to develop trust with my therapist and a sense of my own feelings, my own voice. I had been putting others before myself for so long that it took me a while to find my feet in not doing that anymore.

I spoke a lot about my upbringing. I was angry with my mum. I was angry with Dad too and that was about my overly strict upbringing. Yes, there was a lot of fun, laughter and love in our home, but we were also wrapped in cotton wool a bit too much. We weren't allowed to go to discos or watch EastEnders or anything considered immoral. Would I have given my strict upbringing a second thought if the abuse hadn't occurred and I hadn't been pressured to visit with and act normally around DC? Possibly. We discussed my mum and our relationship in depth. Dad did not seem to see a problem but as my insight increased,

I was able to explain to him, "Dad when you hug me you hold on and it's almost like you don't want to let go of me but when I hug Mum, she's the first to let go."

That's a big difference. Dad needed the hug as much as I did, whereas Mum didn't seem to need it. Mum has since said that she was never hugged or cuddled as a child and is hugely sad that as a consequence she didn't hug me as much as I would have wished.

Then there came a time when I was ready to say everything about DC. I wanted to talk about particular experiences, things he had done and said, how I'd felt at the time, expectations from me, things I hated, the triggers, the trauma. Linda really helped me to break it down. When I told her a particular story from my childhood, I would look at her face and see genuine empathy but not shock. I felt like she could handle anything and that was so important, I felt safe. No extreme dramatics, I'd experienced enough of that from DC's family. She wouldn't say, "Oh wow! Really? That's shocking!" but "That sounds really painful and I'm really sorry you had to go through that Anthea." This was the validation I needed.

About four years into my therapy, I was able to speak about the fact that I had been expected to continue contact with DC. That had been a big part of forming negative beliefs about myself, that I wasn't worthy of protection even when people knew what had happened to me and that my feelings were not valid. Incredibly, even when I was in hospital he would come and see me. That's how arrogant he was, and how lost and confused I was. It never occurred to me to ask him not to come and the feelings when he arrived – dread, gratitude, confusion and guilt due to the dread – were overwhelming. However, the strongest feeling I had though, was physical fear and panic. I was trapped. Again.

In the years since the abuse, DC had really played with my mind. One minute he admitted what he'd done and was sorry, then he would be in complete denial, saying that I was a drama queen and a liar. He did say to my parents that he felt it was his fault I was in hospital because of what he did to me as a child but still nobody suggested to him that he shouldn't come. He and my grandmother had even been at my 30th birthday party in the same year as my breakdown. Paul, guided by the way our family was handling things, even took the children to visit him while I was in Medway Maritime. That was my script: "We're going to dismiss this; we're going to ignore this." I carried that script and Paul used that script as well.

When Paul and I first met he would come with me to my grandparents' house for cups of tea. When the children came along, Paul and I would take them round there. No one really batted an eyelid until afterwards. After I reported him to the police a member of his family challenged me about that. I stood firm. It was difficult knowing we had taken our children round there, but I had changed and was finally able to make healthy, boundaried, self-validating choices.

A year after the breakdown my then church ministers arranged a meeting between DC and my husband and me. At the time I thought the meeting was the right thing to do. I was still battling with forgiveness, which at the time, for me, meant I should be reassuring DC. In addition I desperately needed to believe he was sorry.

The meeting was horrific. Whenever I think about it, I can't believe it happened. He cried and said he was sorry – he was an extremely good actor – and then one of the ministers asked me if I had anything to say. I said nothing. I was only a year into my recovery and was still completely disempowered. The meeting further disempowered me and served only to empower my abuser. He showed (albeit fake), remorse and sorrow but I was too ill to show anything. The power was still all his.

I was informed he felt bad and was going through a hard time too because of the past. Because I was ill, I felt this too was my fault. When a victim is already burdened by immense shame and guilt, to be informed the perpetrator is going through a hard time too will only invalidate their feelings and add to the shame.

One of the ministers wrote to Mum afterwards to say that DC had suffered, describing me as the main victim but that he too had been living under tremendous guilt and shame for years too. The main victim? THE ONLY VICTIM!

This is typical of a perpetrator, many times they will feel no remorse. My grandparents began attending my church and I was asked how I felt about that. My powerless response was, "That's fine, I don't mind," but inside, I was heartbroken. I had lost my sanctuary, a place where I felt safe and connected to God. I shouldn't have even been asked. I wish someone had decided on my behalf to protect and keep me safe. People felt they were doing the right thing by asking me if I minded but I wasn't strong enough to make that choice. I should never have been asked.

Mum was thrilled at her parents' church attendance and how could I upset her when I knew she had been praying for her parents for years? "They're Christians now!" she said. "They're coming to church, and they've been baptised." I'd muster a smile, "Yes Mum, that's really lovely, I'm really pleased for you." Inside I was screaming: I HATE THIS!

There was a lot of re-wiring that needed to go on in my mind. I needed to download new programs and erase the virus that was DC. Once I had acknowledged my wounds, my behaviours, my script, my thought patterns and the reasons for them, I could begin downloading, one step, one thought, one behaviour, and one program at a time. It took years for me to do that, but I was committed to discovering a new, fully functioning me.

It was extremely difficult to talk about the impact that the continued contact had on me. DC manipulating others and myself into continued contact left me feeling violated, I had no free space to heal properly. He was the trigger to the abuse; he would not let me forget.

I was so mixed up. I love my parents dearly and even though I don't blame them, I did question their decision. To talk about them with my counsellor in a negative way was really, really hard but what my therapist helped me to see was that my experience and how I felt, was valid. Whether what my parents did was right or wrong, the impact it had was the impact it had and it was okay to feel the way I felt because that was the way I felt. It is freeing to talk about things without feeling shame. Holding things in causes pain, resentment and anger and this can be very toxic. The anger itself is not toxic. Anger is a valid feeling. What is toxic is not having the freedom and safe place to express it. Having the freedom to say out loud, "Actually I WAS angry with Mum for wanting a loving relationship with a man who was not a good father, and certainly not a good grandfather," was healing and ultimately freeing.

Another thing that made me angry was that we didn't have contact with Granddad Fox as my father's parents split up when my dad was 12. We did have contact in later years, which was really nice, although he died too soon after this was established. But I still needed to work through the anger of why we were left with an abusive DC when there was a nice grandad for us in the world.

It's interesting to consider how much of my breakdown can be contributed to the abuse and how much of it to the continued contact with DC. I think they were equally damaging although at the time, still seeing him, feeling trapped, was the overwhelming trauma. Seeing him and reliving the abuse compounded my feelings of humiliation and degradation. My identity was: She who has been sexually abused. Anthea was diminished, lost for a long time.

As therapy continued, I began to form a picture from the dots of my messy childhood experiences. My therapist helped me understand this dot, that dot, and then to put them together and continue until I could see the bigger picture. As the sessions went on, I began to feel stronger. My therapist metaphorically took my hand and guided me out of the maze. I found the courage needed to turn things around and make life different for myself but also my family. I could see what DC had done and how it had made me feel. Feeling ashamed, guilty and dirty influenced my behaviours and had power over how I negatively perceived self. But once I saw the reality, I no longer wanted to be a victim or be afraid of the stigma associated with sexual abuse. I started to fight back. I didn't want to be held back from living life.

> Do you need to tell your therapist exactly what the abuse entailed? Some victims want and need to do this. But this should only be with a professional who can help you consider the risks, whether you feel safe and have grounding techniques in place and can provide self-care if you experience traumatic flashbacks. Pushing a survivor to talk about what they are not ready to remember can re-traumatise them. Remembering abuse can cause victims and survivors to feel vulnerable and in an unsafe place. Grounding techniques enable you to ensure you're feeling safe in the present.
>
> For a time I tried to dissociate from the trauma. I created an isolating world, an attempt to cope and feel safe. My therapist helped me to observe and describe my world, encouraging me to describe my experiences and environment. Slowly, I reconnected, I no longer compartmentalised, I was ready to unshield my eyes and recognise the triggers that caused me to dissociate. I felt empowered to be the ruler of my own situation, it was liberating!

Many people choose not to talk about their childhoods. There is an unhelpful misconception of: "You just have to grin and bear it, forget it, move on, get on with life." But because of my experience, I have looked at my childhood. I have pulled it to pieces and explored all the nooks and crannies. I have a great level of self-awareness and confidence and now I believe I can reach my full potential. You cannot put a price on being heard and validated. For a victim who holds everything in and lives in a world of silence, to have a professional listen and believe is a balm to the soul.

CHAPTER FOURTEEN

In 2009 – seven years after the meeting between DC and me that had been orchestrated by our then church leaders – things finally came to a head. A friend of the family had died, and Mum was leading a training day at work, so she was unable to attend the funeral. It was in Hampshire and would have meant a whole day off. Her parents wanted her to go and were annoyed when she didn't. They wouldn't let the matter drop. Then, in August, a friend of Mum's from church died. His funeral was just minutes from Mum's workplace, so she took an extended lunch hour to attend. DC rang Mum at work and her boss explained that she was out of the office at a funeral. DC was furious that Mum had gone to this funeral but not the one he had wanted her to attend and wouldn't let the matter drop. Eventually, Mum and Dad went to see him at his caravan to try and sort it out.

Somehow, in the midst of the conversation, DC became adamant that the whole situation was my fault. He said I had lied about the abuse, caused a rift in the family, and was now causing my mum to disobey and upset him. "It's all Anthea's fault," he said. "If she didn't like it, she should have said no. And she lied about being a child. She was fifteen when this all happened."

Mum and Dad were gobsmacked. They couldn't understand how I had been brought into the argument and they were furious DC was trying to change my age, as if that somehow made it more acceptable. Dad reported this in his diary as, "Father-in-law told me, 'Anthea should have said no to his fiddling'." Then Dad added, "I weren't (sic) having any of that." My parents left in a state of shock. They knew they would have to tell me what was being said.

A short while later, I was having lunch with Dad, and he mentioned the incident at the caravan to me. He thought Mum had told me. She was yet to do so and the rage I felt when I heard that once again DC was invalidating the abuse by saying, "She could have said no," and changing my age, as if that somehow made it better, was off the chart.

I had had enough. We had wasted so many years bestowing forgiveness and yet he still was taking no responsibility for what he had done. The occasional "sorry" meant nothing because I never knew when he would blame me again or when he would make up a new lie. I carried on with lunch, not wanting to spoil time with my dad, but when I got home, I picked up my daughter's hairbrush from the coffee table and threw it through the wall. Then I picked up the telephone and called the police to report that I had been a victim of a crime of childhood sexual abuse.

The police were very good and explained that because it was a historical child abuse case, they could deal it with locally. They came to interview me, and Paul sat with me. The police took their time and were thorough. I wanted the truth to be heard. I wanted DC to be punished, to experience just a little of the pain I had gone through. I finally knew that it is not wrong to feel angry, it is not wrong to have a need for vindication.

I told them everything I remembered and showed them my diaries. They asked me, "Have you ever considered you may not have been the only victim?" It hadn't occurred to me, but the thought was worrying. Another thing that stood out from my conversation was when I told them that DC had put his hand down my top, despite me being so young and flat chested. "I don't understand," I said. "There was nothing there." They told me this is common and causes a lot of confusion for the victim. I suppose I thought that an explanation would somehow bring some meaning to it all.

I detailed the last time he abused me in the living room with everyone there and they explained it's another common pattern – the perpetrator abuses in secret to start with but then they want to make it more exciting for themselves, so they take more risks.

It was explained to me that if the case went to court, DC's defence would exploit the fact that I'd had a mental breakdown, been given ECT and been on high doses of several medications. The officers dealing with my case informed me that if there were other victims coming forward, I would have had a better chance of getting it through the court system. But because I was the only one, the best thing to do was to arrest and question DC, in the hope he would admit it and accept a caution which would mean him being placed on the Sex Offenders' Register.

After the police left there was nothing to do but wait. They were doing all they could, but I felt disempowered again. Paul told me he felt proud, that he could see I was no longer powerless, but it took me a while to see that I had taken back control and was moving forward positively.

I needed to face the mammoth task of informing Mum I had called the police and that her father was going to be arrested. I somehow felt I was betraying her, but she said she understood, which was a relief. I was so grateful that this wasn't going to come between us.

It was a waiting game then and my diary entries reveal my extreme anger as I waited for the police to let me know they were preparing the case against DC and the date he was to be arrested.

> September 7, 2009: It's 00:24am, I can't sleep! I feel screwed up the police haven't called yet. I need closure after so many years of tolerating my mum's father. He has manipulated the family, my family, for years. It's still making me feel so angry and resentful of the fact that we all tried to deal with it the 'right way' – naively believing that forgiveness meant having to face him time and time again, being nice, kisses hello, and goodbyes, keeping quiet when Mum went on about their cosy dinners and lunches together or their sloppy texts to each other.
>
> Dear God, if someone had violated my little girl, I'd want to beat them to a pulp NOT love them and seek acceptance from a paedophile! God help me not to dwell on these hurts, I know that all the predicaments we find ourselves in is because of what he did all those years ago. Oh my goodness, this has been hanging over us for far too long. I want a life that I can call my own. I don't want to be a product of past sins that were inflicted on me as a child or even the victimisation. I need to feel like a whole woman. I don't want to feel damaged anymore.

I continued writing the next day:

> Just got off the phone from the police after a two week wait because DC was on holiday, only to be informed we've got to wait another 10-ish days. When I explained that we all feel in limbo, the officer's response was 'In the big scheme of things, I have waited this long, what's another few days?' (He was well meaning but that response was not helpful.) And to cap it all, they are going round there to make an appointment to arrest him because of his ill health! I'm so angry. We have covered up for him all these years, hiding his dirty little secret because I/we felt ashamed, but it is his shame not ours. The police don't want to do the usual arrest because as he is ill, he could drop dead! Do I care? It feels like they are being soft, going easy on him, trying to consider what it might do to him.

> Oh I want to scream, shout and punch someone. Where's the justice? So many girls, woman, men, boys are being violated, damaged, hurt and these scumbags are being tapped on the hands with 'please don't do it again'! As victims we have to pay the price and try to rebuild our lives – the consequences for abusers in comparison are zilch!
>
> I hate feeling powerless. I am so full of regret, it's too little too late, I should have reported him years ago before my breakdown and ECT. Police said his defence would use that against me, yet shouldn't my sufferings go in my favour? My breakdown was a result of suppressing the pain and bottling up the hurts, keeping his secret made me feel dirty. I was robbed of confidence. Without confidence I achieved little. I became introverted, was unable to make friends easily and was bullied. Even though the police were doing all they could, it was healthy for me to be able to acknowledge my feelings and lash out safely in my diary. I was furious that the impact on my mental health could lead me to being considered an unreliable witness. And today, I feel strongly that a change in the system is needed. Victims and survivors who go to court should not be aggressively examined. This only re-traumatises victims and impedes their recovery.

Eventually, a date was set for DC's arrest, and he was interviewed and questioned. He admitted sexually abusing me and was placed on the Sex Offenders' Register for two years. I still don't believe this is enough of a consequence or a deterrent for paedophilia. His life carried on as normal. He even broke the restrictions placed on him and went on holiday without informing the police of his whereabouts. My sister Jo reported him, and the police went to his holiday destination and ordered him back home immediately.

CHAPTER FIFTEEN

I slammed my fist into the punch bag and screamed: "For fuck's sake! Dear God, why are you letting this carry on?" I hit the bag again, harder. "I don't want this to be part of my life anymore!" I roared.

Again and again I hit the bag. "I want to move on!" I shouted. "I want to be well. I want to forget all this. Why is he still saying these things?"

I could barely feel my hands. I slumped on the floor of the garage, tears cascading down my face, my throat burning. But no. This time I was not going to let him put me on the floor. I was not going to let my inner child take another kicking.

I staggered to my feet, spun round and with every ounce of my strength exploded at the punch bag a final time. Enough was enough. I was going to tell DC exactly what I thought.

After he had been placed on the Sex Offenders' Register, Jo went round to see him, to tell him he was nothing to her and that she would never see him again. She was coming to see me afterwards, but she was so incensed when she left that she rang me. "He said you could have said no," she told me.

"Yeah, he trots that line out," I said. "Typical of an abuser. He has no choice but to admit it as everyone knows what he did. But he can't help saying that it wasn't as bad as all that."

Jo was silent for a second. Then she added, "He said you came onto him, Amf."

I felt my heart begin to pump with rage. "Can you believe it?" she said. "He said you started it, 'she started it'. Obviously, I told him, 'You were the adult, Amf was the child'."

"I started it?" I said. I couldn't believe my ears. This was a new low, even for DC. "I started it?" Adrenaline tore round my body.

"I know," Jo said. "Anyway, I'm getting in the car now. I won't be long."

I hung up the phone. Anger burned in my gut. I had been cooking a roast and I picked up a saucepan and threw it as hard as I could. Then

I went into the garage and gave the punch bag hell.

When Jo arrived, I told her I was going to see DC. I rang Paul and Dad at church and told them my plan. They told me to wait as they wanted to come too.

When we arrived at Nan's and DC's house, we entered through the back garden. The two of them were sat there, no doubt discussing Jo's visit. "Nan," I said. "You're not going to like what I need to say to him, so it's only fair to give you the choice to leave."

"No," she said. "I'll stay."

We went into the lounge. The two of them sat down. Nan had her apron on and a tea towel on her lap. DC looked at the floor. I stared at him. "You repulse me," I spat. "Every time I look at your hands, you repulse me. You disgust me."

He stared at the floor. He was spineless. He had nothing to say. I knew that I had taken the power back.

"I was small, defenceless child when you abused me, you were the adult," I went on. "You were the one I was meant to trust. You were the one who was supposed to take care of me. You were meant to keep me safe but instead you did that.

"You told me that I could have stopped you, I could have said no. Well, I did. It was in the front room of your previous house. Family was there and I was on your lap. You tried to touch me, and I said 'Granddad!' under my breath."

He spoke then, and muttering, "I don't remember that."

"Well, I do remember it," I said, "because I'm the one that went through that trauma." I had one final thing to say. "Your lies have to stop. I never, ever want to see you again or hear from you again." And then, without saying goodbye, we left.

Immediately I felt as if a heavy load had fallen from me. I let out a huge sigh. I felt good. Closure? Not all agree with this concept but in that moment that is what it was for me. Standing before the abuser was a self-validating experience. I was no longer scared and no longer damaged. I had found my voice. A new me was emerging and I was no longer dancing to his tune, no longer his victim.

Confronting the abuser may not be right for everyone but I felt I needed to break the control he had. He had victimised me, stolen power from me, shushed me and imposed his shame on me. I was standing in front of the thief and telling him I'm in charge, I'm taking my voice back, but you can have the shame.

Once I had done it the healing process accelerated dramatically. Healing is different for everyone and how you go about it is a personal choice. I confronted DC and am so incredibly glad that I did.

CHAPTER SIXTEEN

As a child I received a lot of messages of love but when I was abused, those messages were drowned out. The negativity was louder than the positivity. Healing from a breakdown and from abuse can take a long time and involves bad days as well as good. I had many dips myself, days when I didn't feel like opening the curtains, washing and going out or doing anything at all. I had more of those days than I can count. It was two steps forward and one step back. At first, I saw those days as failure, but my therapist encouraged me to see that I was allowed the bad days and not to feel guilty about them. I learned that when you go to sleep and you wake up, it's a new day and you can try again. Again, that was empowering because not owning the shame of having a bad day enabled me to find the strength to try again. Before I would have had such a negative mind-set that I would have thought, I might as well stay in bed today too. What's the point? I'm a complete failure.

I believe we are a work in progress until the day we die. It would be wrong for me to say that I've made it, I've got it all sussed and I'm okay. That would not be a true statement. At one point I self-referred to charity Family Matters. They encouraged me to combat my Negative Automatic Thoughts and the therapist recommended I look in the mirror and say: "Anthea is beautiful. Anthea is strong. Anthea is able. Anthea can do it. Anthea is confident."

Not all therapists are in favour of this technique, and I was sceptical, but it worked for me. Not to say I didn't hate it at first – I really hated it. But I persevered because I wanted to be well, and I was ready to try anything. I knew it was time to try and let go of the false sense of self and start claiming what I wanted to be. I stared into the mirror, feeling like an idiot, but I said the words and over time, as I gave my brain new instructions, my behaviour began to reflect what I was telling it.

I started to attempt things and achieve things. I began to feel beautiful and as a result, I felt more secure in my relationship with Paul. It was a big change. In the past I would do my hair and make-up and look in the mirror and wonder why I had bothered. People would say

I looked gorgeous or stunning and I didn't believe them. Discovering that I was a strong person was an exciting revelation. I liked feeling confident, voicing to others that I matter, that my needs matter and that my emotional wellbeing and mental health matters. I felt strongly that my family mattered too. I didn't want them suffering anymore. They had suffered enough and needed to come first.

This is one of the reasons why I encourage others to keep journals. It's encouraging to look back and see how far we have come. It also aids prevention of the re-opening of old beliefs and behaviours. If I want to think for a minute about how far I have come, I remind myself that when I started writing this book, I was able to Google the image of the t-shirt. Why did I do that? Because I knew I had conquered, survived, come through the other side. I was angry at the deliberate offence it was designed to cause but grateful that I was no longer vulnerable, and that evil had lost its sting over my life.

The brain is a powerful muscle. If we exercise it with wrong messages that's how it learns to function. What we tell our brain to think affects our behaviour, so we decline the invitation to the social event, believing that we're not wanted there and won't have a good time. We don't bother going for that interview. Instead, by giving ourselves new and positive messages we can choose to think that we are wanted at the party and will have a good time. We can choose to think that we are equal to the employer and that we both have something to offer each other. If we don't get the job, we can choose to think that it's not personal and that we can take what we have to offer elsewhere. This will affect how we present ourselves in the interview. If the outcome of either situation isn't as we would have wished – we don't get the job, or the party is only okay – then it doesn't matter as much because our self-worth is no longer based on how we think others see us. The idea is to get to a place of thinking: I no longer need other people's acceptance to define me, who I am, what my purpose is.

After DC was arrested and the police rang to update me, they told me some of what he had said. They asked him why he had done it. His response was that I was so affectionate and lovely. For a while I wished the police had not told me that. I found it quite disturbing and felt as if I was to blame again, because I had been seeking cuddles and love, putting temptation in his way. It briefly knocked me back and I wondered if it might not have happened if I hadn't been as needy.

There were times when I felt frustrated with how long the process of recovery was taking and it was explained to me that some victims of childhood trauma don't feel ready to trust someone enough to speak about it until they are retired or even elderly. Although it saddened me to hear this, it also encouraged me to keep trying, to not give up. Yes, it seemed a long, uphill climb but I had a whole life ahead of me to enjoy in what I hoped would eventually be robust mental health.

I chose to go easy on myself and didn't put so much pressure on me to recover. I was also helped by my belief that God wanted good things such as peace, joy, healing, blessings and freedom for me. I wanted those things, I really did. People told me the way I was fighting was amazing. I couldn't see the progress I was making, only all the work I had yet to achieve.

When this book was nearing completion, my sister Sue had a conversation with me about Nan and things from her perspective. The day that DC was arrested by appointment, I had gone to my parents' house with Paul and Jo for mutual support. We wanted Sue with us but at the last moment she decided to go and support Nan. There were various family members at his house, but Sue sat on the floor at Nan's knee, trying to comfort her and when DC returned from the police station, Nan asked him, "Is it true?"

To hear that she had asked this question staggered me. I thought she had known all those years, but maybe had never really known what to believe until he actually signed the Sex Offenders' Register. Another family member then telephoned to see how the arrest had gone and Nan Carey filled that person in and when she got off the phone, DC was furious with her, aggressively informing her that no one needed to know. Sue felt that Nan was totally abandoned and lost that day.

I had been really angry at Nan for years, not just for the things she said to me, but for standing by and defending DC. I had tarred her with the same brush as DC. Listening to Sue, and combining that with my own awareness, I can see that Nan was also affected by DC.

I knew that Sue had taken Nan out for lunch a few times, but it was only in this recent conversation that Sue revealed a lot of sad things Nan had told her such as how trapped she felt. Nan hadn't had a great life. Her own parents were cold, her mum especially, and she always felt a disappointment to them.

My Mum had similar revelations about her own mother in the lead up to her death. She recalls, "I had severed relations with my parents.

Like Anthea, I had tarred my mother with the same brush as my father but then Mum had a stroke, and I was conflicted. I decided to go and see my mum as my husband suggested I might regret it if I didn't. I went to see Mum in her nursing home and there, when I was finally able to have time with Mum away from Dad, I was able to see a different Mum. She spoke a lot about Dad. She died in 2013 and in the last two years of her life, I saw a completely different woman. I am so thankful to God that I was able to have that relationship with her."

Sue also told me that on the day DC was arrested, he told Nan, "It was only the once." He might just as well have said "what's all this fuss about, its nothing."

This is a common response from a paedophile. They have been caught, or have admitted to half of it, so they can no longer deny their crime, but they try and minimalise, brush it under the carpet. It wasn't only once but even if it was, that does not make it okay.

CHAPTER SEVENTEEN

Being a wife and mother has given me the most rewarding experience's but within those roles I continued to search for an authentic sense of self. In 2010, feeling that I was at a crossroads in my life, I enrolled on a Therapeutic Counselling Course. It hadn't been an easy decision. I knew it would be tough, but I prayed and felt in my heart that God was saying I would see other people's pain through His eyes. This happened at a New Wine Christian Conference in 2010. I spoke to Paul about this, and we went back to our tent together to pray for confirmation. The next day Paul was reading a book written by the founder of a charity, a line at the end of one of the chapters read: "You will see other people's pain through my eyes." Word for word. Exactly. It was the confirmation Paul and I had prayed for.

When I embarked on the four-year counselling training course, there was still a part of me that was scared of failure. I wondered if I could really do it and the inner dialogue, the NATs, raised their ugly heads: Anthea, you can't do this. You are stupid, don't do it, you are setting yourself up to fail, will fail! A Counselling Diploma is way above you. Essays, assignments, criteria and exams? Who are you kidding? You won't be able to cope!

By the time I had done a 12-week introductory course, I had an idea of what was ahead of me but would not allow myself to fully digest what the four years was going to entail. If I had allowed myself to think about it, I probably wouldn't have continued. It was a huge undertaking, so I decided to ignore the big picture and instead concentrate on getting through the next four years, one day at a time. I did it one day at a time and as the weeks, months and years went by, I looked back at what I had achieved and began to believe in myself. Manageable chunks were just that – manageable.

Colleagues and peers told me they admired my courage, which of course I found difficult to believe at first. I rarely considered myself as a brave person. But we were gently challenged by tutors if they observed our difficulties in receiving compliments and over time, I learned to believe those positive affirmations.

I'll give you an example of how having self-awareness has improved my life from something that happened a few years ago. I was out to dinner with Paul and Millie, and we were talking about witnessing how prejudice can negatively impact individuals within church life. I made a comment about the quote, "Church is not the building, it's the people," and added that God loves all the Toms, Jacks and Harrys of the church, that he loves everybody, and Millie said, "Even the Antheas." It was just a joke, and she didn't mean it in a derogatory way, but it was a trigger from my old script. The lies I used to believe about myself that no one liked me, and I wasn't loveable, even to God, raced to the surface. I was hurt but also angry that I was hurting and I went sulkily quiet. Part of my inner dialogue was: I can't believe she said that. Doesn't she know that sounds hurtful?

I carried on eating and, thanks to my training I was able to ask myself why it had bothered me so much. I went to get a coffee and when I came back to the table, Paul and Millie asked me what was wrong, and I explained that what she had said had hit a button and triggered past hurts. I then explained to Millie she had done nothing wrong. If I had not suffered abuse and low self-esteem, I would have immediately accepted her comment as a joke and not given it another thought.

Sulking had been a big coping strategy for me, albeit not a very healthy one. One of the daunting revelations whilst on my counselling course was that I could be passive aggressive and a sulker. Even in married life, there were times I would sulk if I didn't get my own way. I was known for my pouting lips. It was hard to admit but I knew this was a learnt behaviour., As a child I wasn't allowed to be angry, it was deemed as disrespectful to my parents. We weren't allowed to express feelings such as anger or frustration. We knew our place. I would go up to my bedroom, shut the door, face back downstairs and mouth, "Fuck you!" and flick V-signs at the door. I'm sure a lot of people can relate to that – so much for Sunshine Bum! Mum and Dad laughed about that when I told them I had remembered this.

We've had our troubles, our ups and downs but Mum and Dad instilled in us from the beginning that family is what matters. Dad always said he wanted to leave a legacy, and they will leave a legacy. When our parents are no longer with us, I know we four – Sue, Jo, Sam and myself – will be close and we'll always be there for each other.

It's what they have created and it's beautiful. I think that's why it's easy to forgive. It's easy to forgive because they are loving, selfless people. They made mistakes, as many do, but they are wonderful, beautiful human beings. Parents don't get a manual and they definitely don't get a manual for when somebody has sexually abused one of their children.

I feel that I have become a much better parent as a result of the therapy and counselling training. Three years ago, I was in the conservatory with the children one Sunday after church and we started talking about the time when I was in hospital. Millie said how much she missed my cuddles and me and I said, "I know, darling, but you had your nanny and grandad and I know they looked after you really well." She burst into tears and said, "I know, but it wasn't you, Mum." She was really upset and had bottled that up for 12 years. Luke couldn't cope with the conversation and left the conservatory.

Recently, Millie said, "There was a time when I hated coming home from school. The blinds would be closed, and Mum was keeping herself to herself. She'd be lying on the sofa. I was very angry. I wanted the house to be tidy and dinner ready. But now Mum's got so much more buzz about her. She's busy, she has loads of energy. She knows who she is and when she talks, she sounds free. Mum knows what she's talking about, her body language shows it. I've literally watched her blossom. It's helped me to be confident too. I haven't always been confident. I was bullied, probably because I was observing, copying, and reflecting Mum's behaviour. We learn by mimicking. But now I feel that Mum is her own woman and I'm going to be my own woman too."

There's a new dimension to mine and Millie's relationship now. We're relaxed with each other; we can talk about anything and laugh so much together. It's a joy and a thrill.

I asked Luke for his thoughts too: "Mum did the best she could, given what was wrong and she never failed to provide me with the best care and love growing up. When I was young, I remember Mum working hard to look after us and the home and Dad working long hours. It wasn't Dad's fault; he did that to provide for us, but it was extra pressure on Mum when she was poorly.

"Living with Mum, who had severe depression and anxiety relating to her experiences, did get hard sometimes. I have ADHD and didn't always understand my symptoms or why things went wrong sometimes. Mum and I clashed a lot. I struggled to understand what was going on and why our family life was like it was. As a kid it scared me.

"When Mum became ill, Dad explained that we'd be going to stay with our grandparents, his parents, and I was happy about this as I loved them and knew Nan would try to fatten me up with her cakes. I didn't understand how long we would be there. I feel for my dad – the woman he loves being hospitalised, having two children who needed their parents and still having to work. He felt bad, I think, because I remember multiple occasions when he bought us gifts and sweets. With Dad working and visiting Mum, there would be days in a row when Amelia and I wouldn't see Dad, and of course we weren't seeing Mum either.

"I remember Dad taking us to see Mum in Medway Hospital which I loved because they had a massive wooden chair at the front door. Random, but I loved it! And it was so long ago that there was a smoking room on the ward. The three of us would spend time with Mum. I remember finding it hard to move around. She was nearly always in her bed or walking around the hospital grounds.

"I've recently been dealing with the effects of everything that happened. I've had depression caused by my desperate need for affirmation. I felt I wasn't good enough and that was why – I didn't see my parents. I find myself looking for acceptance a lot, which I understand annoys most people, especially my current girlfriend! Dad did try to spend time with Millie and me, taking us to the cinema and out for walks. He did the best he could. I wish I had been older when Mum was ill, so that I could have helped Dad, man to man. But I was so young."

CHAPTER EIGHTEEN

"I am not what has happened to me. " I am who I choose to become."

This is one of my favourite inspirational quotes. Learning to be self-aware gave me the tools I needed to make sense of how my past had defined me. Once I gained a level of emotional intelligence, I was able to identify my triggers and reactions to them. Several years ago after a comment like the one Millie made, I would have been triggered and felt hurt for the rest of the day. But I recognised the emotion, told Paul and Millie and was able to enjoy the rest of the evening. The perception of how I saw my world was changing and I was making those positive changes, I felt happy, and I felt proud.

I had to write a dissertation at college and to do this, I looked back over my own therapeutic journey and saw that what Linda was doing in my early years of therapy – the years when I didn't talk much about the abuse or even DC – was showing me genuine empathy, an unconditional positive regard that helped me realise she would never judge me, even if what I said was shocking. In my work, I compared the process to helping a baby take their first steps, you hold out your arms and encourage them. You know they can do it and for me that's it – believing in the client and showing them that you believe in them. If Linda had asked me to talk about the sexual abuse before I was ready it could have potentially set me back and left me feeling unsafe emotionally and mentally. If you make a client walk too soon and they fall, it can put them off seeking professional counsel again.

Today I have a healthy sense of self. I know that I have the potential to reach the goals I set for myself. I have learned to find the solutions to my own problems and not depend or lean on others. I belong and am no longer an outsider. I know my likes and dislikes. I no longer seek the approval of others.

In the summer of 2015 I qualified as a therapeutic counsellor and became an academic – a welcome revelation! Today I can see I have walked the journey from victim, to survivor, and now thriver. I celebrated this joyous occasion with family. Life was going to be a very,

very exciting adventure.

Before my career in Counselling I had attempted various career choices, I have a diploma in skin care and makeup, an NVQ level 3 in childcare, but I had not felt fulfilled or had the confidence to stick at these things. I now love my work. I can competently step forward and bring my dream to fruition. It is extremely rewarding to see lives changed and transformed. This doesn't always happen overnight, but we are all worth having that time invested in us, for the healing process, for the finding of inner peace. Others have shared with me how hearing my story has helped them to realise that they too can survive and find healing. I have received an overwhelming amount of interest of my recovery. Other victims and survivors have expressed it has given them hope and the feeling of solidarity. Our personal experiences can be the key to unlocking someone else's prison.

I did the counselling course because I knew that being a qualified therapist would provide me with the professional tools to use alongside my personal experiences in supporting other victims/survivors of abuse. I feel that if I'd had access to professional and therapeutic support as a child, there is a possibility that I may not have had the breakdown. I was left with large, open wounds. I'm okay now, but it breaks my heart to think of perpetrators robbing children of the chance to live a fully functioning, healed life.

As a survivor and a professional I feel it's imperative to work with other professional and survivors and thrivers, to further increase awareness of complex trauma.

As survivors we are particularly sensitive to the suffering in other victims, an elevated ability if you like, to empathically understand their trauma and emotional pain. There are other successful organisations within the UK whose founders and staff are also survivors of sexual abuse. As a survivor, speaking from experience I can only share how grateful I was to be able to turn to other survivors who knew and understood my brokenness. It took away those feelings of isolation, this was freeing, I would share with them, "At last, someone gets it!"

As a workshop facilitator and counsellor I work alongside other professionals who are thinking about or are already in some capacity, working with victims of abuse and complex trauma by providing them with a unique blend of theory and an informed view from a survivor thriver. We cannot underestimate the power of hearing from the voice of a survivor.

I think how we were as a family, how we brushed the abuse under the carpet; this was all too common in the 1980s and it's a mind-set that prevails today. Who wants to talk about child abuse and sex offenders? It's not a topic people find easy to acknowledge. The abuser could be your next-door neighbour, it could be a friend of the family, or even a member of the family and this can make us feel extremely uncomfortable. Statistics show that many of us live only two miles from a perpetrator. These conversations need to be out in the open more than ever before.

Awareness is being raised of course. Operation Yewtree, which dealt with the historic child abuse carried out by Jimmy Savile, brought the issue into the public eye and as a result, many cases of historic child abuse are being investigated. But it's crucial we get the message out there that perpetrators are not always strangers. In most cases abusers are well known to their victims.

My message is that there is always, always hope. For more than two decades, I could not see hope. The pain felt endless, no matter which way I turned. There seemed no way out. The darkness was everywhere. When my therapists told me, "We hear you, we believe you, we are here for you, and there is hope," it freed me from the captivity of silence.

My healing from complex trauma was a long road but the journey began with someone saying, "You matter. I want to listen to you. I hear you. I believe you and I am so sorry you had to go through that. And the support is there for as long as you need it to be."

Sexual abuse, assault and rape can be devastating and incapacitating. Living with complex trauma and shame can prevent you from living life to the full, whether it's because of the way you think, the way you feel, or because your mental and physical health are affected. All these parts of you can find healing and that is my deepest hope for you.

I was listening to a public speaker on television one day, she is a deeply committed advocate for sexual abuse victims and survivors. She said, "I am glad I was abused, because it made me who I am today." A few years ago if I'd heard that I would've thrown the remote at the TV in anger. Now it resonates. I like who I am today. I love who Anthea is now. I am grateful not for the experience of abuse but for the strength it has given me and who it has made me.

Without the abuse, what I would have had to deal with was the loss of Mum's attention when I was three when the twins came along. This, and Mum's postnatal depression, as well as the impact of her own difficult childhood on me as I grew up, left me insecure and vulnerable. If I hadn't have been abused, I wouldn't have broken down and had to rebuild myself and look at everything including my relationship with Mum. So, I would probably have gone through my whole life with Mummy issues and never been whole or had the level of self-awareness that I have now. The breakdown forced me to deal with everything. Without the abuse the other difficulties in my childhood might not have been enough to push me into therapy.

I know who I am now. I accept I am a beautiful creation, loved, valued, and with a purpose. I suffered for 23 years and took a further 12 years to heal – 35 years in total. Do I feel as if those years have been restored? I can never get them back and when I used to think about that loss, I was hurt and angry. Countless times I wondered who I might have been without the abuse, which parts of me were permanently stolen. I was resentful. And I think it's important for victims to ask those questions and to be hurt and angry over the theft of a carefree mind.

But now that I have reconnected with who the little girl was before I was abused, I am healed. I don't care who I might have been. The connection has been restored. No longer ashamed, I love little Anthea and I love who I am today. That's the restoration I have made and what I am hopeful that I can now offer to others.

CHAPTER NINETEEN

"Amf, he's dead, he's dead!"

The morning of the 11th of March 2019 was going to be a normal Monday like any other. I was in the bedroom fixing my hair before tackling the chores of the day and Paul was getting ready to leave for work when a loud banging on the front door disturbed our routine. We heard a sense of urgency in the knocking. Paul tentatively let my sister in.

"Where's Amf, where's Amf", Jo demanded as she rushed past her brother-in-law. In a matter of seconds Jo was facing a bewildered big sister. I stood in my bedroom wondering what had triggered this tornado.

"Have you heard?" Jo didn't give me a chance to respond. "Amf, he is dead, he's dead!"

"Who's dead, who, who?" I heard myself ask.

"The paedo of course, the paedo, he's dead!"

Paul followed the tornado upstairs and observed the next few moments in silence. What I had spent years longing to hear from Jo, that DC had died and what I had naively expected to feel, joy, just wasn't there. Shock took the place of joy. I felt a rush of adrenaline and my sister and I, not knowing what to do with the energy in the room, embraced and held onto each other and spontaneously jumped up and down. We repeated this in unison, we laughed, and we cried out, "'He's dead, he's dead, the bastard is dead!" (Other expletives were also used.)

Neither of us were in control for those brief few seconds, time had come to a shocking halt. Paul kissed me again and left for work.

Wading my way through chores seemed impossible. Jo said she'd stay with me until she had to collect my niece from school, so I suggested a walk at the beach. From when I was a child and when life has felt overwhelming, the beach has been my go to. The sea is where I feel at home, it is where I feel safe, calm and connected. We walked, talked and hugged. Then we walked some more but this time in silence. I guessed Jo needed to digest the news as much as I did.

Jo recalls that morning: I was on my way to work when I received a call from Mum with the news that DC had died. Mum knew that Amf wanted me to break the news to her and so I made my way to her house. As I drove, I was praying and desperately hoping no one else from our family would call her before I arrived. It seemed the longest 15-minute drive!

I pulled up outside Amf's house, not paying much attention to how I parked the car or even if I had locked it and after running down the garden path, I frantically knocked on the front door. Paul opened it, well half opened it, I pushed the door the rest of the way but felt a quick sense of relief because I could see from the expression on Paul's face that he didn't have a clue why I was there, and not wanting to tell him before my sister, I barged past him and ran up their stairs. I remember Amf stepping out of her bedroom and looking puzzled and that's when I said those words. "Amf, he's dead, he is dead!"

I laughed with surprise at my sister's response. "Who's dead?"

I believe that Amf, like me, couldn't process that this day was finally here, and I didn't want to leave her after that, so I stayed until I had to pick my daughter up from school. She wanted to go for a walk up the beach and it was the windiest of days. We walked and talked, and I remember Amf trying to digest how this would help impact her healing and where things would go from here. I love the selfie we took that day, a reminder of sorts.

How did I feel that day? I felt a mixture of emotions. It felt weird to be feeling something outside of grief. I was feeling relief and I was feeling happy. I was asking myself, should I be feeling the way I am feeling? A weird day but a happy day. I have been with Amf since the day she told me about the abuse and throughout all the years and all the drama from him. So many memories, it all came flooding back. It was like watching a film, but someone had their finger on the fast forward button or was flicking through the family photo album. It felt overwhelming but I knew him dying would mean no more Carey bullshit to tarnish my big sister's life, no more broken pieces to pick up and I felt joyous for her.

When Jo left to go home, I sat alone in the living room with a cappuccino, waves of conflicting emotions washed over me. With each wave rose a new question, questions I knew I might never find the answers to.

For years I had been waiting for this day; aged 92 and DC had finally died. Was this going to be the closure that loved ones had hoped for me to receive? Was his death going to mean complete healing and freedom? For the first time I found myself asking what does closure really mean? The word closure seemed to conjure up feelings of invalidation. I felt anger, not just for me but for my fellow victims and survivors too.

Does closure mean the trauma, my story will be erased? That would be like erasing part of me, wouldn't it? Should I now live my life as though the abuse never occurred? Does closure mean I no longer need to talk about it? Is his death and consequential silence going to be that magic wand moment? If only healing and life for us as survivors was that simple.

Closure comes from the Latin *claus* ("shut") and has many different shades of meaning. Is everything, automatically going to be resolved? Closure does not eradicate the past. Closure does not mean we accept what happened and closure does not put an end to the pain. Our wounds will get knocked and we still need to tend to them. I knew the word closure held no meaning for me; I would never hear from him again and for the time being that was enough.

One of the other questions I pondered on whilst still hugging my coffee was: how do I reconcile grieving the loss of a family member who abused me? When my father's parents died, I felt their loss and I felt immense grief. I cried because I'd never have time with them again, but I was blessed to have been called their granddaughter. Nan and Grandad Fox, they had been through so much, survived a world war, had beautiful hearts and although I still feel their loss today, I can smile when I remember those precious memories. 'Shouldn't' I be feeling sad now DC has gone? That's normally what happens when a grandparent dies isn't it? I felt anger rising up again. Or 'should' I feel relief that the man who once almost destroyed my life, is no longer here?

This should mean it's all over now, shouldn't it…? Then why do I feel like I want to cry? Now holding a half drunk cold coffee, I wondered how different our relationship could have been if DC hadn't abused me? A relationship he stole from me. Today, on hearing the news of his death, shouldn't I be walking round Mum's? Shouldn't it be normal to comfort her and comfort each other? Instead I couldn't handle the thought of being near Mum and being near her pain. He stole that from me, from us.

The news of DC dying felt all-consuming, but I knew I could grab the mixing bowl of emotions and use self-awareness to name each one. I knew I had to give myself permission to feel. To feel anger, sadness and grief for the grandfather/granddaughter relationship he stole from me. When Paul arrived home that evening, he asked how I felt about DC being dead. I explained that I couldn't yet describe the feelings but was prepared to do the work, to explore and process and I reassured him I'd be okay.

The three weeks leading to the date of his funeral were particularly hard; experiencing traumatic and vivid flashback's, ones I had not experienced for many years. I didn't want to revisit the abuse, rehash the past but his death was a monstrous trigger. I was choosing to face the triggers head on, the alternative, avoidance, was not an option. I opened the toolbox and used the tools that had helped me turn my breakdown to a breakthrough. I reminded little Anthea she was safe, that DC couldn't hurt her anymore and that she would grow into an awesome and fierce woman.

Although DC had died it felt as though he had taken up free lodgings in my head; my thought-life leading up to the day of the funeral was consumed with so many questions. Do I go? Do I stay at home? If I attend his funeral, will it benefit me in any way? Will seeing his hearse trigger me? Will I regret not seeing that box being lowered into the ground? I should go to support Mum, after all, he used to be her dad. Maybe seeing him buried will be a touch of that closure loved ones are hoping for me to find?

These were questions I was not prepared for. For years I had said that when DC dies, I would be attending his funeral, I made the decision believing I would need to see him lowered into the ground. A very long chapter closed but now I wasn't sure what to do. I told Paul and my family I'd decide on the day.

Was DC's mere existence and breathing oxygen inexplicably keeping the memory of the abuse alive? Now he's dead will all the memories be buried with him? Of course I knew the answer to that last question. No, but I also knew that I was now the one alive and had already done the work to take back control. Although I had taken the power back, after he died and for a brief moment, it felt as though my grip was loosening a little.

The Funeral.

"You fucking paedo, you fucking paedo" I heard myself shout in sheer rage at the top of my lungs as I launched towards the hearse.

I woke on the morning of the funeral and decided almost instantly I needed to go. Listening and trusting in my gut instinct I phoned Jo to tell her I'd be going. Paul had booked the day off work on the assumption I might want to go. No smart funeral attire but I chose to wear jeans and a warm jumper. I put a winter coat on, grabbed my scarf and book Shh… and Paul drove me over to the cemetery where my sisters were waiting. My parents arrived soon after, my mum had also made the decision to go that morning and we were all parked near the cemetery gates just before 10am, plenty of time for us to compose before the hearse was due to drive past. I could watch the procession and burial and then leave quietly, I told myself.

DC decided he didn't want a funeral service; his house was at the back of the cemetery so it would be just a one-minute slow drive to his final destination. We all wondered if he had a level of awareness of his own wrongs. Maybe enough to influence his choices when he was making funeral plans. No service he said, straight to the hole in the ground. He explained to family members helping him with the final arrangements, "I don't want any of that lot knowing the date of the funeral," he demanded. Our wondering's were brief. DC did not want us there, not because of any shame or guilt he may have felt but because he wanted to hide behind those grieving. Grieving attendees paints a picture of someone who was worth grieving for. DC did not want the truth at his funeral, declaring who he really was on his day of rest.

Paul, Dad, Mum, Jo, Sue and I stood close together waiting and it seemed an unbearably long wait. When I heard the hearse approach my body begun to uncontrollably shake, tears welling up, the procession neared to where we were standing and what happened next, I can only describe as an out of body experience.

"You fucking paedo, you fucking paedo." I heard myself repeatedly shout with sheer rage and at the top of my lungs. As I lurched towards the hearse there were other expletives and hand gestures, but my parents and sisters swiftly came to my side, circling themselves around me in the vain hope they would be able to console and contain me, but I broke free, and the outburst continued.

My family followed me and was, I'm glad to say, successful in their second attempt to hold me still and as the shame begun to hit me of what I had just done I collapsed into the circle of family around me and cried. This was to be the last time I felt shame in relation to DC.

It was a reaction and definitely not a carefully considered action. My intention was to watch him being lowered into the ground and then quietly walk away. Seeing as many funeral attendees as I did, as well as observing a handful of grieving family members was definitely a trigger but my needing to be there took precedence over what he wanted, over what his grieving family members wanted. I didn't see it as a selfish act but was indicative of how far I had come and showed me that I really did have a healthy sense of self-worth.

Paul and my dad shared how they felt and responded to my outburst. Paul said he turned around so his back was facing the procession; he did not want to see his wife upset in that way. He said, "you were releasing years of pent up and powerful emotions." Dad said he looked on protectively but didn't like seeing me that way. Dad has never seen me explode with so much rage, but I reassured him he would never have to witness seeing me that way again. Mum and Sue shared how they both felt relieved for me because I had the opportunity to release everything and were proud that my voice was heard. They were right, after I had gotten over the shock of what I had done I found a cathartic release and somehow it felt cleansing.

I quickly jumped in our car, passenger seat and hid. Sue joined me seconds after, she sat in the back seat, drivers side, and began to snigger. "Sue! You can't laugh, someone might see you," I said as I looked outside to see if anyone had noticed.

"Sue, why are you laughing?"

"Amf, I can't help it."

"What do you mean you can't help it?"

"Amf, you should have seen yourself!" Sue re-enacted what she had seen and heard me shout. "Amf, I'm just not used to seeing you like that."

By that point I was already going over and visualising the scene, but Sue's laughter got me, she told me in no uncertain terms that I was not to feel ashamed but proud. "I am so proud of you, Amf, none of his lot are ever going to forget that, and if there was anyone there who didn't know he was a paedophile, they do now!"

My tears were soon replaced with laughter, and I quickly hid my face in my scarf and the tears of pain, frustration and anger were no more. God, I love my sisters! My sisters, to this day like to remind me of 'that' scene and we end up giggling every time.

Jo recalls the day of the funeral: My memories aren't really that vivid. Amf was undecided if she was going to DC's funeral, but I felt quite excited. The anticipation of who was going to be there. Who was going to support DC? I felt happy at the thought of no one being there for him. The prospect of watching the hearse go past and with no procession, made me feel happy but people were there, and I felt gutted.

I was looking at Amf while we were waiting for the hearse to arrive, a wait which seemed to drag on and on, as though DC was wanting to annoy us all, one last time.

We could hear the hearse arriving and it was about to turn the road where we were waiting when I spotted one of DC's sons, I felt sick and diverted my eyes back to Amf. I didn't want to take my eyes off her and was wondering if she was going to be okay and handle seeing DC go past? Is she gonna explode? Get back in the car? I didn't know what to expect and was taking it, one second at a time. The anger was welling up, but I felt determined to maintain decorum for Amf's sake. It irritated the hell out of me that there was a substantial procession behind the hearse, and I hated it.

Amf was quiet and then she wasn't quiet. The highlight of that funeral was Amf's explosion and one of DC's sons reaction. "Leave the poor bastard alone." It was only about 20 seconds of something you'd see on an episode of a very popular TV soap, but it was a side to Amf even I had never seen. Then there was another wait, I can't remember what the hold-up was, but I just stood there thinking, will this bastard just not go in the ground? But the inevitable happened and he did, I was happy, that was it, the end and goodbye. Is it wrong to feel happy that someone has died?

When Jo said she was happy DC had died I found her words comforting, she was normalising my own feelings, her message was, it is okay to feel happy and relieved he is now dead. I think we can all think of historical characters who have committed unimaginable crimes against humanity, and we were right to rejoice when they died. Let's not pour more shame on victims and survivors for feeling relieved when the abuser dies. We need to come alongside and comfort them for the loss of a relationship they were entitled to but never had. The wicked are not to be grieved for or remembered with fondness and it is normal to feel free, the abuser can no longer harm us or anyone else, that is something to be incredibly happy about.

Once the mini graveside service was over and almost everyone had left, I got out of the car and caught up with a couple of family members who were there for similar reasons as me, to see a chapter shut down, we comforted each other a little and they left to go home. The grave diggers were waiting to fill in the hole, but my family had spoken with them beforehand; they stopped and waited for me to do what I needed. With Dad and my sisters by Mum's side she stood and read to DC from the note she had handwritten and then threw the letter along with a stone, on top of his coffin.

For Mum, the stone was symbolic of all the pain he had caused her and her family, pain which was now to be buried with him. After Mum had walked back to her car Jo gave me the signal and I rushed to DC's graveside alone, I was aware the grave diggers were eager to get on with their job and I had no interest in prolonging the events of the morning! I briefly glanced at DC's coffin and without uttering a word I threw my book on top of him, said thank you to the grave diggers and ran back to the car.

DC had silenced me, now death had finally silenced him.

CHAPTER TWENTY

"Everything can be taken from a man but one thing: the last of the human freedoms – to choose one's attitude in any given set of circumstances, to choose one's way."
VICTOR E. FRANKL, "MAN'S SEARCH FOR MEANING"

Did I choose to be born? No. Did I choose to be abused? No. Can I choose the path I walk? Yes. Trauma was ever present, trauma was a time traveller, trauma was an all-consuming darkness trying to destroy and devour me.

Have you ever tried to sit down and watch a really scary movie, but it was far worse than you had expected, so switched it off? The horror movie was my reality and DC was the director, he was manipulating the stage and controlling the scenes. Images I was unable to unsee, the replay button was stuck, and the scenes were imprinted in my mind.

How did I survive the abuse? One question of many that I am asked. Love certainly played a significant role in rescuing me. Family and friends persistently showered me with love, and slowly but surely I began to trust their messages of: you are worth so much more than what happened to you. DC had made my universe all about him, but messages of love turned my universe around and as I bravely glimpsed at myself through the eyes of loved ones, DC's dominant presence began to fade. Seeing myself through the eyes of loved ones shed light on my strengths and self-loathing turned to self-love. Self-sabotaging almost killed me; self-love saved me. I allowed myself to feel proud of what I had suffered and the work I had done to overcome. I worked hard and learned how to put trust in my own strength and fought with all I had to realise my own potential.

No, I am not what happened to me, the sexual abuse does not define me, I was born, and it did happen, but I am free to be in control of what my existence means. My attitude towards the sexual abuse was and is mine to determine. Do I hold on to the potent negative emotions of pain, anger and resentment? Only 6 short years I knew freedom and innocence. Do I continue to hate the thief? Surviving and how I survived was up to me to decide. I allowed myself space and time to self-validate, I am a victim of sexual abuse and once I had worked through those layers, I asked myself the following questions: Do I want to remain a victim? Do I want to remain DC's victim? Or do I want to break free? Can I muster up enough self-belief and courage to grab life by the horns and fight for a meaningful existence? Dare I even contemplate thriving? That last question scared the hell out of me. Feel the fear and dare to believe that I can do it, dare to turn my life into one that is worth living. With fear and excitement I took a tentative step towards hope and before I knew it, I was experiencing a little of freedom and believe me, once you have had a taste of complete freedom after decades of having none, you want more, so much more, freedom became addictive. What a beautifully healthy addiction freedom is.

How did I find freedom and how am I experiencing freedom now? The day I faced DC in his living room was a conscious decision to grab freedom with both hands. I was giving the director, DC, the boot, he was no longer going to have a say in how my life looked and how scenes were going to play out and I was adamant he wasn't even going to have a small role to play in my life. DC was sacked! I became far too bright for his horror show, so I walked away and starred in my own award winning movie. I was holding a bright, crisp white piece of paper and I began writing. My hand was shaking with fear, but I wrote. A new day was dawning, I was singing my own song now! It felt like a rebirth. The growing pains were hard, but I was growing.

Qualifying as a therapeutic counsellor, supporting other victims and survivors and standing in a room full of people to share my story. I was getting taller, and my new story was turning into quite a thick book. I was wearing my big girl boots and each step I took towards freedom was another step away from the grip of the past. I was becoming that awesome and fierce woman I had promised little Anthea. What I had failed to tell little Anthea was that aged 46 she would feel brave and free enough to learn how to ride a motorcycle!

I had finally found me. Jumping on a motorcycle and riding up a dual carriage way on the afternoon of my CBT (Compulsory Basic Training) I cried tears of joy in the helmet. "Well, there she is! Hi there, Anthea" I cried. In that moment I realised that I had, at last, enough sense of self to actively seek out a life's long dream. A dream now fulfilled. With a determined spirit I went for it and a flame within me was ignited with the sound of that Kawasaki Z 650, the bike I learned on at the training school. When I'm riding my bike, a Honda CB650R, my spirit feels alive, and that newfound experience of living life and freedom is mine! All my senses come alive when I'm on my motorcycle, the smell of petrol, the vibrations and sound of the engine, the views when I'm riding in the country or tasting the sea air when we are riding along the southeast coastline. It is exhilarating and when I'm out on the bike I often remind myself of how far I've come and say things like: and you thought you wouldn't amount to anything. Check you out, wearing your leathers and getting a good lean on in that tight bend.

All my biker buddies will confirm I'm a little obsessed with the chain on a motorcycle, as soon as I see a sparkling, well-oiled chain and it doesn't necessarily have to be mine, I feel instantly happy. It got me to wondering where this new obsession had come from. A few days ago I was trying to explain my enthusiasm for motorcycle chains to a friend and she described it for me beautifully. "You were chained to your past; chains held a negative connotation and were symbolic of repression but now a chain gives you freedom." The only chain that gives me freedom.

People gave their lives so that we might have freedom, what a powerful word and one that stirs powerful emotions. People died for freedom, a beautiful gift that I needed to believe I was worth having. Is that it now? All done and all okay now? Heck no! But freedom is feeling excited about writing my story. Freedom is knowing who I am and doing who I am. Freedom is flying. Freedom is feeling free to love and trust again. I am free to let people in. I am free to feel beautifully overwhelmed at all that life has in store.

I am free to choose living. I am free to choose hope for a bright future, so bring it on!

THE END

Printed in Great Britain
by Amazon

20938048R00061